FATHER
GOD

DARING TO DRAW NEAR

DAVE PATTY

CONTENTS

INTRODUCTION

God uses many words to describe himself, but one is stunningly personal—*Father*. Not just *King* or *Creator* or *Lord*, but amazingly, unexpectedly, even intrusively, *Father*. You can't hear this word without feeling some kind of emotion, either warmth toward your own dad or mistrust because of how he disappointed you. The word *father* never enters our thoughts alone; it arrives either laden with blessing or loaded with regret.

It is not surprising, then, that your view of this member of the Trinity can be easily distorted. You don't have another Jesus, or another Holy Spirit, but you do have another father, and your experience with him changes the way you see God.

If your dad is your hero, you may feel you don't need another father, or see God as a cosmic version of your dad, which is a box much too small for God.

If your dad is your heartache, he can fill your heart with disappointment and debris, leaving no space for a Dad of a different kind.

In either case, allowing God to reshape your definition of his fatherhood into one that is distinct from your dad can have a profound and utterly transforming effect on your life. If you had a closer connection with God as *Father*, you would:

- have a clearer sense of purpose and direction
- feel more loved, accepted, and valued

- have more energy and motivation
- be more resilient to rejection
- be more grounded and rooted during hardship
- feel less need to defend yourself
- be less impacted by other people's demands
- have a better relationship with your earthly dad
- be a better father or mother to your children
- have more confidence in the future
- experience less anxiety
- be released to reach the full potential of who God created you to be

Does this sound a bit like oversell? Actually, according to Scripture, the potential riches available in the fatherhood of God exceed even your highest expectations.

Although I've glimpsed just a small part of this treasure, my personal experience of the transforming impact of God's father heart has profoundly changed my life. After watching many others radically changed by a deeper encounter with him, I've become convinced every believer needs more of God's father heart. If you join me on a journey through the pages of this book, I believe you will experience your heavenly Father in a new way that will transform your life, deepen your relationship with your earthly dad, and profoundly bless those under your care.

In the chapters ahead you will learn about four streams of God's father heart and why your soul will either grasp for false substitutes or starve without these resources. You'll see how your dad's behavior toward you imprinted you to either connect with God as Father or experience emotional distance from him. You will find that some of the troubling behaviors you have not been successful at changing are actually driven by what I call "father deficiencies."

Most importantly, you'll discover what you can do to fill those voids, and how both Jesus and the Holy Spirit are working right now, today, to draw you into a deeper relationship with your Father.

Are you ready to respond to their call? I believe you will be blown away by what the Father has prepared for you—if you will dare to draw near.

1

THE INVITATION

The note Martin's teacher handed to him at school was confusing. "Don't come home today. Your father has been in an accident. Go straight to your aunt's house."

Martin sucked in his breath sharply and felt his heart start to pound. What did this mean? Like most young boys, Martin idolized his dad. He was strong and capable, all the things Martin wanted to be when he grew up. Sometimes he felt a certain distance between them, like his dad didn't know what a father was supposed to do. But his dad was a man's man, and that mattered most. His work repairing high-voltage wires was dangerous, but that just made him more of a hero in Martin's mind.

What happened? Is he hurt badly? Without a phone there was no way to reach Mom, so Martin did the only thing he could. The wind whipped his jacket as he leaned into the frosty air and ran all the way to his aunt's house.

She knew no more than he did. They both waited for news. His mind made the strange connection that this was Children's Day in the Czech Republic where he lived. Maybe children needed a special day because they were small and helpless—that's how he felt as he waited. Small and helpless. He sat up straighter, trying to fill out the coat he still hadn't grown into.

What if Dad had fallen? What if something had fallen on him? What if he was never coming home? Martin quickly put that thought out of his head, willing it not to be. Not on the day of children. A twelve-year-old boy still needed his dad. Especially this twelve-year-old.

The phone rang. He heard his mom's strained voice on the other end. "He's in the hospital," she said. "He slipped while working on a transformer and came into contact with a high-voltage wire. The doctors are doing all they can."

"Can I come see him?" Martin shouted into the phone, unaware he was yelling. "I have to see him!"

His mom hesitated before responding. She seemed distracted. "No, that wouldn't be good right now. Just stay with your aunt and wait."

The phone went dead. She had forgotten to say good-bye.

Now there was nothing to do but wait. Stay and wait. He flipped through the television channels at his aunt's house. There were just five. He couldn't stay on one for more than a few minutes. There had to be something that would drown out the noise in his head. He turned up the volume. Maybe it was possible to drown out his noise with more noise.

Sleep evaded him most of the night, and it seemed like an eternity before he saw the gray light of morning. Another phone call interrupted breakfast. Mom's voice sounded weary on the other end. "No change," she said. "You stay there; I need to be here with Dad."

He felt his fear well up in anger. "That's not fair," he cried out into the phone. "I want to be with Dad, too. Can you ask him if he wants to see me? Can I come later this afternoon? Is he going to be okay?" His questions tumbled out quickly, leaving no space for an answer. When he ran out of words, his mom was quiet. "Just wait, honey. I'm doing all I can," she said, her voice thin and strained. "I'll call you later."

At least this time she said good-bye. But no call until evening, and no change in the news. Then another night of tossing and very little sleep. What do you do when you don't know the answer to the biggest questions in your life? "Is my dad going to be okay? And why won't anyone let me see him?" The hours stretched on forever, and even the noise from the TV was not enough to distract him.

Martin didn't believe in God. But even though he didn't exist, this might be a good time to ask for his help. "God, help the doctors. Help my dad," he prayed. Though it was the first time in his life that he had prayed, his words bubbled up from the depths of his heart. "Don't take him from me," he pleaded. "I'm too young to be without a dad," he said out loud, hoping someone would hear.

Forty years of Communism in the Czech Republic had tried to erase any memory of God, but it seemed there was nowhere else to turn. For some reason it felt better to pray, even if he didn't believe in the power of prayer. Maybe God would answer. Maybe God would help him. Perhaps he would even start to believe.

Another night passed without news. Finally in the morning, his mom walked through the door. She hardly looked like herself. Her face was pale. She didn't look him in the eye.

Martin ran over to her and grabbed the sides of her coat without thinking. "Where is Dad?" He tried to search her face, but she looked away. Martin wondered why his mom refused to look at him and why she kept staring at the corner of the room. Why were those tears forming in her eyes?

"Martin," she said, her voice breaking as she spoke his name. "Your dad's not coming home. The high-voltage shock was more than a human can handle." Now her voice dropped to a thin whisper. "He died instantly . . . three days ago. I just didn't have the strength to tell you."

"NO!" Martin screamed, pushing his mother back like one who had been betrayed. "He can't be gone. I need my dad!" Brushing his way past her, he ran out the door. The rage and loss blinded him with tears, but still he ran, stumbling down back streets as he cried, and hoping no one would see.

"My dad is gone forever!" He couldn't yell the words out loud, so he screamed them in his mind. As he ran, his body shook with sobs. Straining to see through his tears, he stumbled on the rough sidewalks. Then the prayer from the day before began to mock him. That peace he felt afterward must have been an illusion. When he called out to God for help, Dad was already dead. If God existed, he had been silent. Why hadn't he done anything? That kind of God was not loving, but cruel.

As he ran, Martin vowed in his heart never to believe in God. It was obvious he could not be trusted. Maybe no one could be trusted.

. . . .

I met Martin three years later.

At that time I couldn't make sense of his sullen disengagement. It's hard to know what story lies behind a closed face or an angry heart. Martin sat across from me in our small group discussion but spent the entire time looking at the floor. Wanting to improve his English, Martin had signed up for a summer English camp led by our team of missionaries in the Czech Republic. He knew the camp was sponsored by a small local church, but he didn't expect we would sit in a circle and actually talk about God.

The God who didn't exist. The God who had betrayed him.

I was still disoriented by the challenge of learning a strange new language and culture. My family and I had moved to the northeast corner of the Czech Republic just nine months earlier, shortly after the fall of Communism. God burdened our hearts for the young people of the region, and we wanted to do everything we could to introduce them to a personal relationship with Jesus Christ. We called our ministry Josiah Venture, in honor of the young king who turned his nation back to God.

There were few believers at that time. In our town of 100,000, I could only find twenty-five young people who were followers of Christ. The Communists had built the city from scratch to house workers for the nearby steel mills and coal mines. Militantly opposed to God, they were proud of the fact that their central planning did not include a single church. Now this atheist regime was no longer in power, and new doors had opened to reach the next generation.

Were their hearts open to hear? I could tell by looking at his body language that Martin's heart was closed and locked as tight as a vault.

Our little church had a youth group of five at the start of camp. At the end of the week I invited everyone who was interested to gather at our house. "It will be a lot like camp, only every week," I told them. "We'll talk about God and how you can have a relationship with him."

I guessed there would be some who were curious about this strange American family. But still I was not prepared when over sixty showed up for the first meeting.

From my vantage point, pressed up against the old cast iron radiator, I looked out over our small living room that was suddenly full of young people. I saw curiosity, skepticism, students who had never heard anything about God. Many were in animated conversations, using coarse language I hadn't learned from my Czech tutor. Then I spotted Martin in the corner, quiet, looking down. I hadn't expected him here.

Martin liked basketball. After one meeting, Todd, one of the missionaries on our team, offered to teach him some new moves. They began to connect over sports, and on a long walk home after a game, Martin told him the story of his dad's death. Suddenly a lot of things began to make sense.

For Christmas, Todd gave him a Bible and a basketball. "You can only accept one if you promise to read the other," Todd told him. He held both in his hands. It felt like a trick to Martin, but he reluctantly accepted.

The basketball must have meant a lot to him, because Martin kept his word about reading the Bible. He started hanging around after youth group, asking me questions about what he had read that week. Underneath his hard, angry exterior was a boy longing for connection with a father figure. His questions gave me a glimpse of that heart, and I found myself drawn to him. My own young kids grew to love him in spite of his rough edges. Our entire family began to pray earnestly for Martin's salvation.

The road to faith is often a long one for the youth of the Czech Republic. Almost a year later, Martin cornered me in a back room after youth group. With his typical intensity, he blurted out, "Can you tell me again how I can have a relationship with God?" We had been through the gospel many times before, but I was happy to review it again.

A few minutes later I had my hand on his back as we both bowed in prayer. With halting words and a great deal of emotion, Martin confessed he was a sinner and put his faith in Christ. I could hardly contain my excitement as he prayed. When he finished, he grabbed me in a joyous hug. He had been working out in the gym that year, and I thought he would crush me.

In a moment I realized something profound: this young man was a new believer, but he still desperately needed a dad. Without saying a word, I promised myself I would be that father for him.

It was a noble promise. But I didn't know how significantly I would fail.

2

FATHER HUNGER

Your father is more important than you realize.

It doesn't matter if you are in daily contact with him, if he lives far away, or if he is no longer alive. There is hardly an area of your life that is not touched by his influence. Social science researchers have attempted to discover the extent of this impact, but the results can be overwhelming. A group of counselors and educators in Canada formed a special organization to compile this research, naming it the Father Involvement Research Alliance, or FIRA. Their insights on the effects of father involvement in children's lives are profound:

- School-age children of involved fathers are better academic achievers. They are more likely to get As, have better quantitative and verbal skills, and perform a year above their expected age level on academic tests.
- Father involvement is positively correlated with children's overall life satisfaction and their experience of less depression, less emotional distress, less fear and guilt, fewer conduct problems, higher levels of self-reported happiness, and fewer anxiety symptoms.
- Adolescents who strongly identified with their fathers were 80 percent less likely to have been in jail and 75 percent less likely to become unwed parents.

- On the other hand, in father-absent homes, boys are more likely to be unhappy, sad, depressed, dependent, and hyperactive. Girls who grow up in father-absent homes are more likely to become overly dependent and have internalizing problems such as anxiety and depression.[1]

This already looks like a significant list, yet the full results of their findings take fifty-eight pages to document. It almost sounds like an Internet ad for some new remedy, one that can cure hundreds of ills. We are rightly suspicious when we see those kinds of claims. But you better take note of this one: *Every one of us has a father, and we all have some kind of relationship with him. Your father's influence on you is greater than you know.*

As you read this, you may feel an immediate sense of grief. Like Martin, you may have lost your dad through death, divorce, or permanent separation. There is nothing you can do to get him back, yet every day you feel the loss of his guidance and care. Most people around you are not aware of the depth of that vacuum in your soul. While you may function well on the outside, you constantly feel your father deficiency and have to invest significant energy to compensate.

Perhaps your dad was around but not accessible. You knew he cared about you, but the pressures of work or the pull of his hobbies kept him distant, unengaged. Perhaps he didn't know what to do or didn't have the confidence to wade into the messiness of "father engagement." For whatever reason, he missed you. And you still miss him.

Dr. Margo Maine is a clinical psychologist who specializes in counseling young women with eating disorders. Wanting to do her best to help women caught in this destructive cycle, she read all the literature she could on the different causes and treatments. Then one day when treating a patient named Barbara, she had a flash of insight and asked about Barbara's father. Soon it became clear Barbara was desperately hungry for emotional connection with her dad. "She thought that having a different body would please him," Maine wrote, "so she had dieted, lost weight, over-exercised, and purged, masking her pain and emptiness."[2]

This prompted Maine to find out if her other patients with eating disorders were driven by similar needs. She discovered that "when dads are uninvolved, absent, or inconsistent, their daughters experience what Barbara was describing—a deep, unrelenting father hunger." In her insightful book *Father Hunger*, she writes:

> All children long for a close, loving relationship with their fathers. They are born with an innate drive to connect with them. Children literally yearn for this connection. . . . When this normal craving is satisfied, children are likely to grow up feeling confident, secure, strong, and "good enough."
>
> Often, however, this yearning is not acknowledged and the need for a bond with the father grows, causing self-doubt, pain, anxiety, and depression. *Father hunger* is a deep, persistent desire for emotional connection with the father that is experienced by all children. . . .
>
> Like physical hunger, unsatisfied emotional hunger does not disappear; instead, it grows and grows. Adults who have not found a way to relate to their fathers or resolve their feelings of loss may continue to suffer this hunger indefinitely. They bring their longing to new relationships when they become spouses and parents. In this way, father hunger is passed down through generations.[3]

Some people may not recognize this emotional hunger, since it often hides beneath the surface. But it can, without warning, explode into anger when the raw nerves are touched. Let me illustrate this dynamic:

Speaking in an interview with *Vogue* magazine in 2012, singer-songwriter Adele made it clear she had absolutely no interest in keeping a relationship with her father, Mark Evans. He abandoned the Grammy-winning singer when she was three, and he had recently sold a story to *The Sun* detailing his personal alcoholism and split from Adele's mother. "I was actually ready to start trying to have a relationship with him again," Adele told *Vogue*. "He's ****ing blown it. He will never hear from me again. . . . It makes me angry! To come back after ten years and be like, 'Maybe her problem with men comes down to me.' It's like, 'F*** off! How dare you comment on my life?' It makes my blood boil. . . . It blows my mind," she said. " 'I love her so much'? Really? Why are you telling me that through a newspaper? If I ever see him I will spit in his face."[4]

When her dad read the interview, he was confused. "I can't believe she said that. It's devastating. I don't know where it's come from," he said. Later in the same conversation, he confessed he didn't own any of Adele's albums, nor had he seen her perform live. "When she sings, it's so beautiful," he said, "but it brings back too many memories. It's too painful. There's so much regret on my part—regret that I wasn't a better father to her. I let her down badly, and I wish I could turn the clock back and do things differently."[5]

It is clear from Adele's reaction that she wasn't interested in mending fences.

Others try to anesthetize the pain by lowering expectations. Rap singer Drake grew up without a father after his dad divorced his mom and left them both when he was five. When he opened up about his relationship with his dad, he insisted everything was resolved. "Me and my dad are friends," the star told *GQ* magazine.

"We're cool. I'll never be disappointed again, because I don't expect anything anymore from him. I just let him exist, and that's how we get along. We laugh. We have drinks together. But I spent too many nights looking by the window, seeing if the car was going to pull up. And the car never came."[6]

It seems Drake has absolved his father of all parenting responsibilities so he can have some kind of cordial relationship with him today. But what about the boy inside who is still sitting by the window, still waiting for a dad who never came? And what about the engaged father he needs today?

Psychiatrist Dr. James Schaller noted a common theme in his counseling sessions: the depth of hunger men and women feel for fathering. "Even those in their sixties and seventies have told me of the hunger and longing they still feel," he wrote in his book *The Search for Lost Fathering*. Schaller observes:

Often the need is hidden, like a deep river of water flowing under the surface. The hunger may be out of sight but it is never gone. I have heard hundreds of people tell me what they want from life. After we get beyond the superficial they say something like, "I want my father to call and talk to me" or "I want my father to stop drinking and come home. I need him so much."

After more time, the deepest waters break through to the surface. The hunger, longing, and disappointments begin to come forth. "I wish my dad were alive." "Dad, I feel so weak without you." "I wish my dad weren't sick so I could lean on him the way I used to." And so it goes.

Most of these people are highly functioning members of their communities. They are respected in their relationships. They are responsible employees. Nevertheless, they obviously have unresolved pain associated with their fathers. They thirst for "father water." They have been left with a void, an injury, a psychic thirst that only a father can quench. I am becoming increasingly convinced that this is nearly universal.[7]

Schaller recognized that none of us can afford to ignore the presence of our father thirst. He concludes, "You may be surprised to see the extent of your father's role in your most cherished relationships, your vocation, your satisfaction with life, and your experience of God."[8]

This was the thirst I often sensed from Martin. As more young people began to put their faith in Christ in our atheistic city, I saw it in them, too. So many came from broken homes or lived with distant dads who hardly knew their children. The boys were growing into men without a strong masculine presence to guide them. The girls were becoming women without the protective care of an engaged and loving man. As they put their faith in Christ, I longed for them to grow up to be the men and women that God had created them to be. But how could that happen without a father's care?

I tried to be a surrogate dad to them, and my wife, Connie, showered them with a mother's love. Some of them made our house their second homes; several lived with us for extended periods of time. These relationships were deep and meaningful.

And yet it often seemed we were pouring our love into a vacuum that could never be filled. As a surrogate father, I also became the object of their father dreams and disappointments. The best I could give did not seem to be enough to fill the void, so I would feel a constant cry for more. Then, without warning, the tables would turn and I would become the lightning rod for their frustration and pain, as if I were the one who had caused the hurt they held inside. This was confusing and painful for me.

On top of this, I was trying to be a good father to my own three young children. This was more challenging than I had guessed. I often found myself at a loss to know what they needed from me. Was my father care supposed to be different from my wife's mother care, or just another version of the same? Of all the things I could give to my children, what did they need the most from me?

One evening when we were sitting at dinner, Martin appeared in the kitchen. There had been no knock, no warning, just a muscular young man leaning up against the kitchen door frame grinning at us. "What's for dinner?" he asked, obviously expecting to be invited to join us. My wife gave me a panicked look that needed no words. I had been gone for several days, and we needed time alone as a family. And this was not the first time Martin had just "shown up" in the house. His unexpected appearance made her nervous and uncomfortable.

I caught my cue and got up to meet Martin. "Hey, let's talk at the door," I said. Ushering him out, I explained that we needed this meal alone as a family. I reminded him to knock before coming in. I told him we loved being with him but needed the freedom to say no at times. The conversation didn't go well. It was as if I were kicking him out of the family, as if his dad were leaving him again. He left hurt, and I returned to the meal frustrated. I don't remember anything from the rest of that evening with my family.

Later on that week, Connie shared her concern that I was disengaged with our kids. When I gave the excuse that it was just some recent weariness and stress, she gently shared she had been feeling it for some time. This was hard to hear and even harder to accept. I felt I was failing as a father, both to my biological children and my spiritual ones. On top of that, I was missing my own dad. Why was I still feeling a need for something from him? He was far, far away, and I was a grown man. Wasn't I supposed to be able to make it on my own? Feeling I had nowhere to turn, I went downstairs to my study and made a decision that would change my life.

I decided to study the fatherhood of God.

3

FOUR GIFTS

I had an exceptional father. His engagement and care gave me resources that most of the young people I was working with knew nothing about. But instinctively I knew even the best father was a poor one in comparison to the greatest Father of all. Somehow I would need to discover the nature of God's father heart before I could even evaluate what I had received from my dad—as well as what I was trying to give to my kids and those in our ministry.

A quick word study of God the Father turned up more references than I could count. I needed some way to get to the core, to find the essentials that held the entire picture together. Then I had an idea: Why not look at the Father's relationship with his Son, Jesus? Since they were in perfect communion, enjoying a relationship unmarked by sin, theirs should be the benchmark for a perfect father-son relationship. I remembered a key story in Scripture where we actually overhear the Father talking to his Son at his baptism.

Opening my Bible to Matthew 3:16–17, I read this: "As soon as Jesus was baptized, he went up out of the water. At that moment heaven was opened, and he saw the Spirit of God descending like a dove and alighting on him. And a voice from heaven said . . ." Stopping before the end of the verse, I tried to picture the scene in my mind. Jesus is at the start of his ministry, virtually unknown to the people gathered around John the Baptist. Keep in mind, Jesus had not performed any miracles, nor had he yet distinguished himself as a teacher.

Though John the Baptist had been speaking of someone greater who would come after him, Jesus has yet to publicly make claim to his calling as the Messiah. This is the moment where it all begins, as we see all three members of the Trinity revealing themselves to the watching crowd, each relating to the other as we look on.

This is, in some ways, a private interchange between a father and his son. On the other hand, it is a deliberate public announcement to all who are listening, a declaration of a father's heart to his son, proclaimed out loud so everyone will hear. Note carefully what he said: *"This is my Son, whom I love; with him I am well pleased"* (Matthew 3:17, emphasis added).

How would you like to hear that from your father? What would it be like if he were to say out loud, in public—without hesitation or embarrassment—for everyone to hear, "This is my son. I love him. I am well pleased with him!" And there you would stand, taking it all in. Of course, if you are a daughter, it would sound like this: "Hey, listen everyone! This is my daughter. I love her. I am well pleased with her!"

How would you feel? What if your father's announcement was not based on something great you had done, or hard work you had completed, but was rooted solely in the strength of his relationship with you and the depth of his passionate love for you? Can you imagine what that would be like? I sat for a while and tried to let the power of the Father's proclamation sink in. I tried to feel what it would have been like to hear this same message from my father. Then I realized this is not the only time in Scripture when we overhear the Father talking about his Son.

Turning to Matthew 17, I began to review the story of the transfiguration. In this account, Jesus had withdrawn to a high mountain with three disciples—Peter, James, and John. Somewhere near the top they sensed a strange light, and they saw the face of Jesus lit up like the sun. Even his robe had been transformed into garments of shining white. Out of nowhere, two other figures appeared and started to talk with him. Somehow the disciples could tell (perhaps from the conversation?) that they were Moses and Elijah. Overwhelmed with surprise, Peter wanted to capture the moment and preserve it. He tells them it is good for all of them to be there—the understatement of the year—and quickly adds a personal offer to build three shelters, one for each of them.

"While he was still speaking," Matthew wrote, "a bright cloud covered them, and a voice from the cloud said . . ."

Here it comes. A voice from heaven, the Father's voice, making an announcement about his Son for all to hear. What does he say? *"This is my Son, whom I love; with him I am well pleased. Listen to him!"* (Matthew 17:5, emphasis added).

Does this sound familiar? Do you remember these words? With the addition of one phrase at the end, it exactly matches what the Father said at the baptism of Jesus. I caught my breath at the significance of what I had just read. If you only overhear a father talking about his son twice, in widely different circumstances, and both times he says the same thing, wouldn't those words represent the core of his relationship with his son? I wrote down on my paper, "The four gifts of the Father"; and then I began to list them:

1. **Identity:** "This is my Son"
2. **Love:** "whom I love"
3. **Pleasure:** "with him I am well pleased"

I was stuck on what to do with last phrase: "Listen to him!" These words didn't occur in the baptism, yet they were added here.

What was God's father heart expressing? I looked back at the rest of the passage for clues. The context seemed to indicate Jesus was receiving something very significant from his Father. Like in some regal ceremony, the spotlight shone on his face, his garments lit up with a supernatural glow, and amazing special effects focused our attention on Jesus at center stage.

And why those two guests? Jesus was the heir to the prophecies of Moses about a coming deliverer, the fulfillment of the law Moses recorded. He was the embodiment of the power of Elijah, who had skipped death and was to signal the arrival of the Messiah by his return. Their presence perfectly framed his place as the Promised One.

As the Father gloriously ushered his Son into his rightful place, Peter foolishly tried to get all three of them into a place of *his* design—namely, three homemade shelters. His plan seemed perfect to him, but it was far from what the Father intended.

"Listen to him!" the voice said reprovingly to Peter. It's as if God was saying, "You are not the one calling the shots here, Peter." The Father defines and defends his Son's place. I tentatively put down the fourth gift, hoping other Scripture would confirm it.

4. **Place:** "Listen to him!"

These four gifts seemed important to me, but I had no idea how significant they would become. I wondered if a different viewpoint would lead to the same conclusions. "If this is what the Father says about his relationship with the Son," I thought, "I wonder what the Son says about his relationship with the Father?" Going back to my word study, I focused in on the Gospels and noticed a heavy concentration of references to the Father in the fifth chapter of John. Turning to read the entire passage, I found Jesus in the midst of a very difficult and pressure-filled argument with the religious leaders.

He had just healed an invalid on the Sabbath, and the Jewish leaders were furious. Jesus defended his actions by saying, "My Father is always at his work to this very day, and I too am working" (John 5:17). This is an unusual defense. Jesus could have argued that the healed man had been crippled for thirty-eight years and should not be left to suffer another day. Or perhaps he could have contended that telling an invalid to get up and walk on the Sabbath wasn't really work. He could have reminded them of his popularity and the potential backlash from the crowd, or made some counter threats of his own (we all know he had some burly angelic warriors on his side).

Instead, when Jesus needed a firm place to stand, he stepped back into his relationship with his Father. "I work because my Father is working."

Right away I spotted the first gift—*identity*. Jesus knew *who* he was because he knew *whose* he was. He knew what to do, because he knew to whom he belonged. His Father was working, so he was working too. The Jews immediately understand this as an identity statement. John records, "For this reason they tried all the more to kill him; not only was he breaking the Sabbath, but he was even calling God his own Father, making himself equal with God" (John 5:18).

You can hear the angry protest of the Jewish leaders. "No way. If you are God's Son, you are automatically someone extremely great. That's not fair; you can't make a claim like that!"

Don't miss this: Identity gives value. As the Son of God, Jesus would automatically have astounding value and worth. And when identity is given rather than earned, it is secure in the midst of accusation and pressure.

Such was the case with Jesus, who was not moved at all by their violent anger. The Jewish leaders were trying to kill him, but he didn't back down, didn't run, and didn't hide. Neither did he respond with anger or an attack of his own. Why not? Because Jesus was rooted in who he was as God's Son. He could rest secure in his identity. So, in spite of the threat on his life, Jesus said, "Very truly I tell you, the Son can do nothing by himself; he can do only what he sees his Father doing, because whatever the Father does the Son also does" (John 5:19).

Identity brings clarity. It lays down boundaries to activity and creates clear pathways through the chaotic sea of possibilities and the clamoring agendas of others. What do I do today? "Don't do anything by yourself. Do whatever you see your Father doing." Then the passage takes a surprising turn. "For the Father loves the Son," Jesus continues, "and shows him all he does. Yes, and he will show him even greater works than these, so that you will be amazed" (John 5:20).

Did you catch it? The second gift of the Father—*love.*

Okay, this is a bit strange. Picture yourself in the same situation. Some powerful people want to kill you for trying to help an extremely needy man on the wrong day. You are making your public defense. The first interchange doesn't go well, and the angry emotion of your accusers has jumped to a dangerously new level. What do you say now? "Hey guys, I need you to know that my dad loves me a lot."

Really?

Often we associate love with soft violin music and dreamy sunsets. We think of a warm, romantic feeling or a candlelit dinner. Love is half-voiced, a bit passive, soft, or maybe tender.

Not this father love. It is fierce, passionately strong, full of initiative and masculine engagement. Father love is not afraid of self-disclosure (he "shows [the Son] all he does") and not ashamed for everyone to know ("you will be amazed"). Not at all like a soft rose petal, father love is a strong shield, the kind of protection you hide behind when the arrows start to fly.

If father identity gives value, father love is what brings security. My Father cares deeply about me. I'm not alone. He shares his heart with me so I know him and trust him. When I hear the rejection of others, it does not destroy me. Why? Because I am accepted and loved by my Dad. Father love surrounds me on all sides and creates a place where I am truly safe.

Now it made sense to me that Jesus would pull out this gift when the threats and accusations mounted. Without a deep sense of security, it would be impossible to stand his ground without launching into an ugly counterattack. His Father's love provided that safe place. It is one thing for a father to declare his love for his son, and another for a son to say it of his father. This only happens when love has been fully received, when it has penetrated and left its mark, when it has not just been heard, but experienced.

But Jesus still wasn't finished with his defense. He continued, "For just as the Father raises the dead and gives them life, even so the Son gives life to whom he is pleased to give it" (John 5:21). Do you see the connection? Now he is jumping to the fourth gift, the gift of *place*. He tells how his Father purposefully makes space for his Son to join him. This is like a farmer who slides over on the seat of the tractor to make room for his boy. "This is my place, but beside me I will make a place for you. I'm driving this powerful rig, but you can drive, too."

When that boy is older he will probably drive on his own, with his father piloting another tractor in a different field. He may be entrusted with managing part of the farm and negotiating grain deals when it comes time to sell, "just like Dad."

A good father makes a place in his world for his son or daughter and passes on to them privileges that are his. This is exactly what is happening when Jesus says, "For just as the Father raises the dead and gives them life, even so the Son gives life to whom he is pleased to give it. Moreover, the Father judges no one, but has entrusted all judgment to the Son" (John 5:21–22).

Wow, this goes even further! In some areas the Father makes a place for the Son by letting him join him. In other categories he actually steps out of his responsibilities and fully entrusts them to his Son. Judgment belongs to the Father, yet he has entrusted it to the Son. This delegation of responsibility does not come because the Father is overworked or can't manage his to-do list. Rather, it is a gift to his Son, a purposeful empowerment that gives him place. Why does he make a place for the Son? He does this so "that all may honor the Son just as they honor the Father. Whoever does not honor the Son does not honor the Father, who sent him" (John 5:23).

If identity gives value and love brings security, what does place bring?

Honor.

Why do we covet certain positions and work so hard to earn various titles? Why do labels like "the first . . ." or "the only . . ." or "the top . . ." mean so much to us? Why do we feel so adrift when our roles suddenly change or we lose our place in a set of relationships or on a team?

Place brings honor. Place gives us authority and the ability to act rather than be passively pushed around by others. Place creates boundaries of belonging in our life and keeps us from disappearing unnoticed into the meaningless mass of humanity. This is the confidence Jesus expressed as he continued to defend his calling, a calling he did not create, but one he received. Watch the clarity, confidence, and authority Jesus expresses because his sense of place flowed from his Father:

> "Very truly I tell you, whoever hears my word and believes him who sent me has eternal life and will not be judged but has crossed over from death to life. Very truly I tell you, a time is coming and has now come when the dead will hear the voice of the Son of God and those who hear will live. For as the Father has life in himself, so he has granted the Son also to have life in himself. And he has given him authority to judge because he is the Son of Man" (John 5:24–27).

What about the third gift—*pleasure*? Looks like he skipped that one, right? I wondered for a moment why that was the case until I read on and was amazed at what followed. Jesus said, "By myself I can do nothing; I judge only as I hear, and my judgment is just, for I seek not to please myself but him who sent me" (John 5:30).

There it is! The third gift: his Father's *pleasure*.

Our own selfish interests or the selfish interests of others often distort our judgment. Why was the judgment of Christ so clearly just? Because of the nature of his motivation. His only desire was to please the Father, and this motivation gave undistorted energy to his actions.

Seeking to please someone who is important to us and desires what is truly good can be a powerful energy, one that propels us toward the right destination. Everyone has energy and motivation. However, it is often burned up in futile self-protection, or channeled toward selfish and destructive ends such as our own status, glory, and power.

This is what Jesus was referring to later in the chapter when he said to his accusers, "How can you believe since you accept glory from one another but do not seek the glory that comes from the only God?" (John 5:44). I looked back on my sheet with the list of the four father gifts.

1. Identity
2. Love
3. Pleasure
4. Place

The Father's Heart

These were exactly the same four things Jesus stressed when speaking of his relationship with the Father. Amazing! But why these particular four? Why were they so important?

I took out my pencil and added a few observations from John 5.

1. Father identity gives *value*.
2. Father love brings *security*.
3. Father pleasure gives healthy *energy and motivation*.
4. Father place brings *honor*.

Looking at the list, I had two contradictory feelings, each fighting the other for more of my attention. "This is awesome!" I cried out to myself. And then, "This is disturbing," I muttered under my breath. It was awesome because these four gifts are exactly what all of us need. It was disturbing, however, because I had no idea how to take them from the paper and actually make them a real experience in real people's lives.

Mine included.

4

THE IMPRINT

When you were young, you were like hot wax or wet cement. Your identity was pliable and moldable as you worked to answer the basic questions of who you are and how you should relate to others. Because of the unique role of fathers, your interaction with your father as you grew up left an "imprint" on your life, much like a handprint in cement, or a bicycle track across wet pavement. Once the cement hardens, this imprint is very hard to change.

In my case, and in contrast to most of the young people I was working with, I grew up in a strong Christian home. My parents spent their entire lives serving God and investing in the spiritual growth of others. What they taught in public matched what I saw in private. Their example made the Word of God come alive to me as I watched it practically lived out at home.

Reflecting on the four gifts of the Father, I began to review memories of what I had received from my dad that shaped me as a young man. Comparing the words of Jesus with experiences of my own helped me understand them better.

Identity

I was always very proud of my dad and who he was. The important fact that I was a Patty always gave me a feeling of great worth. After all, my dad was the Executive Director of Overseas Christian Servicemen's Centers. His title was quite a mouthful, but I looked for opportunities to drop that information casually into conversations, hoping the other kids would be impressed.

If my dad was someone great, then I must be important too. I think every kid wants to be proud of their dad. As kids, we intuitively feel connected to our dad's character and accomplishments, and we instinctively sense his identity somehow rubbed off on us.

Dad's words had special weight as well. My older sister was just a year and a half ahead of me, and her strong personality and gifting set the bar quite high. As she wowed people with her quick engagement and captivating insights, I struggled to learn my colors and put together complete sentences. Everything she did was lightning fast. I was hopelessly slow.

The contrast was easy to see and compare, and I'm sure many people did. But I don't remember any response beside my dad's. "You don't have to be a smart boy," he said, sitting beside my bed one night, "just as long as you are a good boy. That is what is most important to me as your father." As I think of those words today, they sound a bit hokey, but that's not what I felt at the time. I heard recognition of my limitations without judgment, as well as a challenge for who I needed to be. I had my marching orders from Dad.

As a young child I seemed to have only one volume when I spoke—very loud. Maybe it was the challenge of finding my voice next to a gifted sister, or perhaps I was trying to be heard in a home that was always full of guests. I'm sure there was temptation to make fun of my lack of social sensitivity, but my dad saw potential in it.

"You are going to make a great preacher someday," he told me. Of course I immediately wanted to know why. "Because you have a strong voice, and preachers need a voice like that." I sat up straight and ran those words through my mind. A preacher. Could I be someone important like that?

My dad's words of clarity about who God had made me were repeated many times and in many ways over the years. He was realistic about my shortcomings and not afraid to confront areas where I was failing. But I always felt his belief in me and his confidence in who I would become.

Many others spoke words of identity to me, but I cared *most* about what my dad thought. Who he was and what he said to me seemed to give my life context and orientation. This was a huge gift—a father gift, given over and over again with the special potency fathers possess.

Maybe you, too, can think of identity gifts your father gave you. If so, you know his words affirming your identity met a crucial need in your life as you grew up and prepared you to be able to hear words of identity from your heavenly Father when you came to know him.

However, in Martin's case, his father was gone. The fact that his father was distant when he was alive further complicated matters. How could this huge deficit be made up? How could I somehow pass on to Martin what I had received? On top of that, I had to admit what I had received wasn't always enough for me either. In many ways I was like my dad, so the identity messages received from him were a good match. But it was harder to get oriented in areas where I was different.

For example, Dad grew up on a farm and loved to garden. We raised lots of vegetables together; the garden was a place of great connection and learning. But left to myself, I would rather spend my time building something out of scrap wood or dreaming up some new "invention" than tending the garden and making things grow.

I was more of a builder than a farmer. Yet when I acted like a "builder" I felt a little lost, without clear affirmation and direction. Dad was giving me all he had, yet in some areas his identity messages didn't seem to totally match the person I sensed I was created to be. As I grew older and began to develop skills and capabilities outside my father's experience, I often felt unsure, like I was pretending to be someone I wasn't. His father gifts were a huge asset. At the same time, he was limited and imperfect, so those same gifts were incomplete.

The "father imprint" became clearer when I reflected on the second of the four gifts.

Love

I was absolutely sure my father loved me. I could see it in his eyes and sense it in the way he cared for us as a family. At the same time, he wasn't great at expressing it. He grew up in a divorced family without siblings or a mom for many of his formative years. This left its mark and affected the way he related to us. For example, physical affection was not part of his communication style, and neither were verbal expressions of love. I remember deciding to give him a hug when I left for college and feeling uncomfortable for both of us. I know he was filled with strong emotion, but hugging him felt like hugging a board. I never remember hearing him speak the words "I love you" when I was growing up.

My relationship with him is very different today, as my dad has continued to grow and mature. But the father you grow up with as a child is the one who leaves a lasting mark while the wax is hot.

If in the area of identity I had many father gifts, in the area of love I had a significant father vacuum. Since I admired and respected my dad so much, I unconsciously responded by turning off these areas of my heart. If my dad wasn't expressing his love to me, then I must not need it. Worse, as I learned the hard way, I didn't know how to express love either.

I couldn't believe what my ears were hearing. Since my girlfriend and I were dating long distance (before the invention of Skype,

FaceTime, or Facebook), we communicated most often through cassette tapes. It was a one-sided conversation, but I liked it better than handwritten letters because I could actually hear Connie's voice.

This time, as I played her latest cassette tape in my car, I desperately wanted to interrupt and stop that voice. She said, "Dave, you are a really great guy." The tone of her words was strange. "But I feel so little emotion from you. I love you, but when I try to communicate my love, it doesn't seem to penetrate. It's like your heart is stone. And I'm getting nothing back from you. No expressions of love, no engagement from your heart. I wonder if you know how to love."

What was she saying? I heard her words but immediately felt defensive. "That's not true. I care for her a lot," I said to myself. "She is being too demanding."

The voice on the tape ignored my inner protest and kept talking. "Maybe you will find a girl who doesn't mind that, but that girl is not me. I am not willing to continue in a relationship where I don't experience love. I can't change you. But I can take responsibility for my future. So I am ending our relationship. I hope you have a great life, and I wish you the best."

Okay, now this was bad. I felt betrayed, like someone had kicked me in the stomach and left me out on the street to be run over by the next truck. In spite of the fact that I was driving to work, I immediately turned the car around and headed straight for home. I had to find a phone—had to do *something*. My best friend, David, was living in the same city as Connie. I would call him. He could help me.

As soon as he picked up the phone, I cried out, "I've got to talk to you! Connie just broke up with me. She said I don't know how to love, and she doesn't want to be in a relationship like that." My words tripped over each other as I spilled my horrible tale.

"So she did it," David said, with a sigh of amazement. "Wow!"

What did that mean? "Did you know about this?" I retorted.

"Yes, she talked to me about you last week."

"And what did you say?" I asked, hoping he had defended me.

"I told her to dump you. Dave, she is right. You're doing a rotten job of loving her. She deserves better than that."

I couldn't believe it. No way. This can't be true. "Some best friend," I thought as I hung up.

But by the end of the day I realized David was just the kind of friend I needed. An honest friend. I was caught. I didn't know how to love. And it wasn't easy for me to receive love.

Now I couldn't turn it off, couldn't ignore it. The stakes were too high. Later that evening I found the courage to call Connie. Her voice was distant and guarded. "You're right," I said earnestly, "I haven't been loving you, but I want to learn how. You have accurately described my problem, but there is another solution than breaking up. Would you give me a second chance?"

She said she had to think about it.

It took a while to convince her I was serious. In the end she did give me a second chance—and a third, and a fourth. My wife, Connie, has been helping me learn how to love for twenty-nine years now. I am very grateful.

There are two common expressions of a father vacuum. You saw the first one in my story. Without father gifts, an area of our heart dries up and dies. We become paralyzed like the Tin Man in *The Wizard of Oz*, unable to move ahead in life because we have no heart. To manage the father vacuum, we turn off those needs, ignore them, and then lose life and feeling in that part of our hearts. We wall off that part of ourselves and become like a corpse, lifeless and unresponsive.

Often others are much more aware of these dead spots than we are. When they encounter them they are confused by our lack of engagement and response. They don't understand why we can neither give nor receive in this area of our lives. Since one of the characteristics of deadness is lack of feeling, we are often equally confused by their feedback and response. "What is their problem?" we think to ourselves. "There's nothing wrong here."

The other symptom of a vacuum is a constant pull. Think about the vacuum cleaner you use at home. Whenever you push the ON button, a fan spins up and creates a vacuum in the inner chamber. Several feet away, this chamber is connected by a long tube and a small opening to the outside world (which also happens to be your living room). You know what happens here! The vacuum created in the chamber pulls on anything and everything that happens to be near the end of the hose, trying to suck in something that will fill the void.

Filling the vacuum is a good thing when this includes some dirt and dog hair you were hoping to get rid of. Of course, as long as the fan is on, the inner chamber won't be satisfied, and the vacuum cleaner hose will keep pulling on whatever is around it—like the bottom of your pant leg or that earring you just dropped.

This is the second expression of a vacuum—the constant pull to fill what is lacking inside. I could see signs of this in my life as well. On the outside it looked like I didn't need love and didn't care to give it. But on the inside my natural needs found a path to the surface through other channels.

Heading into puberty, I was totally surprised by the power of my newly emerged sexual desire and attraction to the beauty of women. More than just impacting me physically, it seemed to touch some deep longing in my soul. Though I was much too self-conscious to ever admit it, there was a deep desire to touch and be touched, a desire that seemed full of potent energy and thirst.

Trying to satisfy our legitimate needs in inadequate and sinful ways creates a deeper thirst and sends us into a cycle of ever-increasing pain and disappointment. This is what fuels addiction and bondage to sin. At the same time, our basic need is very real. The vacuum in that inner chamber must be addressed. I took out the paper where I had listed the four father gifts and added these observations from my reflection on identity and love. I wrote:

> All of us have been marked by what we experienced from our fathers. This imprint shapes us long after we have left the home. Where we have received **father gifts**, we will find healthy **giving** and **receiving**. Where we experienced **father vacuums**, we will find **deadness** (the corpse) and **pulls** (the vacuum cleaner).

I could see examples of these dynamics in my own life and in the lives of those I worked with over the years. But I still needed to do some more thinking about the third and fourth gifts.

5

PLEASURE AND PLACE

My dad was the director of a mission organization. That meant he was an important man. But his role of overseeing scores of missionaries in distant countries often sent him on long trips that took him far away from us. Knowing what I know now, I am even more impressed with my mom. She never complained and never did anything to lower our view of Dad when he was absent. That didn't mean it was easy for her, or any of us, while he was gone. We always counted the days until his return.

Walking home from grade school one glorious spring afternoon, I checked the calendar in my head: "Two weeks until Dad gets home!" This thought filled me with excitement. Yet a couple of weeks felt like an unbearably long time. I wondered what I could do to fill the space until his return. An idea flashed through my mind: "I wonder if I can do something that will surprise him!"

What I didn't have in mind was the kind of surprise when someone jumps out of a dark stairwell at you, or the surprise you experience when you discover your water pipes sprang a leak while you were away for the weekend and the basement is now flooded. No, I wanted to surprise him with something great—something amazing that I could accomplish with my own two hands, something that would make him pleased, proud, and delighted that I was his son.

Turning the corner into our yard, I noticed our property resembled a jungle. With the onset of spring, the foliage had furiously launched into grow mode, and all of it needed attention. Our bush-es were much too large and in need of a haircut. The flowerbed was growing a healthy crop of weeds. Our once-dormant lawn was now encroaching onto the sidewalk, and the entire yard needed a good mow.

I knew Dad would walk this same path from the driveway to the back door in just two weeks. Knowing how much he loved farming, he'd appreciate whatever effort I could muster to beautify our yard.

Hmmm, I wonder if I could prepare a surprise.

Mom found me elbow deep in the flowerbed when she got home from shopping later that afternoon. I battled the weeds there until evening. Over a late dinner I asked Mom if she could pick up some flowers at the market for me to plant the next day.

I rode my bike to school in the morning so I could get home faster when classes ended. After finding the hedge trimmers in the back of the shed, I began to beat back the new growth; I had to borrow a small stepladder from the pantry to reach the higher limbs. The project was a mixture of fun and sweat. Shaping the bushes was great fun, but it was much less enjoyable picking up all those tiny branches and making sure they all made it to the trash.

My back was sore. My hands ached with blisters. But I could already see the difference, and the thought of Dad's arrival spurred me on. The next day I mowed the lawn and edged the sidewalk.

Next I gathered the leaves still left over from fall and the trash blown in by the winter winds and stuffed them in the overflowing trash bins. Every day brought another change, more progress. The two weeks flew by as I worked hard every afternoon, transforming our unkempt yard into a place of beauty. At least, that is how it looked to me. I'm sure the bushes were a bit lopsided and the edg-ing job was not quite straight. I probably didn't get the right flowers planted in the flowerbed, and I could never mow the lawn with the precision Dad had.

I knew he would notice, but would he be pleased or disappointed? What would he say? D-day finally arrived. I was nervous as I rode my bike home from school. Mom had already gone to the airport to meet his plane. All that was left for me to do was anticipate his arrival. I heard our car pull into the driveway. Taking a deep breath, I ran out to greet Dad. Pulling one of his small suitcases, I walked a few steps ahead of him as we rounded the corner of the garage and headed toward the back door. I was looking at one thing.

My father's eyes.

He took two steps down the walkway and then stopped. I watched his eyes scan the lawn, then catch sight of the bushes at the edge of the house. There, I could see it on his face. That look of surprise.

"Wow!" he exclaimed. "The yard looks grrreat!"

He took another step forward. "The lawn is so even," he said. "And those bushes look like they have been trimmed by a professional."

His eyes brightened, "Those flowers are beautiful, and . . . has this sidewalk been edged? Who did all this?"

I dropped my head sheepishly and slowly raised my hand.

"Dave? You did all of this? By yourself?"

I nodded silently, not wanting to say anything that would keep me from hearing his full response. Just then, Mom chimed in. "Yes, and it was his own idea, I didn't even ask him. You wouldn't believe how hard he worked on it. He's been out here every afternoon for two weeks."

"Dave, that is amazing!" Dad exclaimed. "Not many young boys could handle a difficult challenge like this. And all by yourself? I am so proud of you!"

There. I got it.

My dad's pleasure and delight. And in that moment all the long hours were so very worth it. All my effort had won the reward. Dad was really, really pleased, and I was one very happy boy.

Pleasure

Do you see it? The third gift: father *pleasure*. We heard it in Matthew when God the Father announced he was "well pleased" with his Son. You know it, too, because this desire to please our fathers is built into every one of us.

Notice how a healthy desire to win my dad's pleasure gave me energy and motivation to work hard and overcome difficulty. Remember what we observed from Jesus? He kept going under pressure because he was seeking the approval of the Father. Father pleasure can be like a healthy inner engine that propels us forward toward valuable outcomes, in spite of obstacles and opposition.

I recognize that for some, this approval seems impossible to attain.

Take Daniel, for example. In spite of the fact that Daniel was one of my best friends in high school, I never enjoyed spending time with his family. His dad led a fruitful ministry to college students and possessed a powerful personality. A big man with a booming voice, he could captivate a crowd with his passionate teaching and deep convictions.

But I often heard that same voice raised in anger, dressing down one of his kids.

I remember one time when they asked me to join their family for a day on the lake with their ski boat. Daniel was backing the trailer into the water as his dad shouted directions from the side. "Back up slowly. No, I said 'S-L-O-W-L-Y.' What's your problem, Daniel? Can't you hear?"

Daniel was getting nervous and shifted his foot to the brake. "Don't stop now, you *idiot*," his dad yelled. "Can't you see the boat is barely in the water?"

I tried to make myself smaller in the front seat. Daniel eased the boat farther into the water and brought the car to a stop. Then he sat still, looking forward. I didn't know what Daniel was thinking, but it felt like he was trying to figure out how to keep from making another mistake. A minute or two passed when his dad barked, "What's going on in there? Are you two going to make me launch the boat all alone?" "Teenagers," he muttered under his breath. "Always thinking of themselves."

We scrambled out of the car, trying to guess what we were expected to do next. The fear of another verbal blow made us both anxious, and we started to make stupid mistakes. A wrench dropped in the water, and we couldn't find it. The boat drifted too far forward and scraped on some rocks. Each new failure was like pouring gas on the fire, and the intensity of Daniel's dad's anger increased.

"How can you be so stupid?" His dad's words were punctuated by pauses for effect, and his gaze was withering. I could see Daniel didn't have a chance. There was no way to answer this question without provoking an outrage. And there was certainly no possibility to win his dad's approval. The sun was shining, the lake was calm, but I have no memory of the waterskiing we did that day. I was too shell-shocked by what I'd experienced from Daniel's dad. I couldn't imagine what it must have been like for Daniel to face this every day.

In the last chapter we talked about *father gifts* and *father vacuums*. What Daniel received that afternoon was a *father wound*. A vacuum occurs when there is an absence of father resources; a wound is what happens when a father gives the opposite of what the child needs. Instead of giving identity, he dismantles the child's worth; instead of communicating love, he streams rejection. Instead of pleasure, there is caustic disappointment; and instead of giving place, a father takes it away.

Just like a physical wound, a father wound is deeply painful, even debilitating. After that dreadful day on the lake, I came to understand why, at times, Daniel would go rigid and withdraw deep into himself. Sometimes unexpected little things would suddenly cause his walls of self-protection to snap into place.

Daniel hated to fail. Even when his dad was not around, he tried to protect himself from doing anything wrong. When it seemed he had failed, he would disappear inside himself, trying to somehow fix it before coming out of his shell again. I could almost see the self-punishment going on inside, the inner attempts to make sure this failure didn't happen again.

You remember from the last chapter that father gifts produce healthy giving and receiving. Father vacuums produce deadness (the corpse) and pulls (the vacuum cleaner). Here we see the first expression of a father wound—walls of self-protection we erect to protect ourselves from future hurt.

Unhealed wounds are raw and sensitive. Even a light touch to this vulnerable spot can send jolts of pain to the rest of the body. A hard hit would send you through the roof. It is only natural to try everything you can to keep a wound protected. When we exhibit this self-protective behavior, it doesn't make sense to someone looking from the outside—unless they know about the wound.

Not long after I finished college, I had a couple of moles surgically removed from the skin on my chest. They had been bothering me for some time, and I didn't want to risk the possibility of cancer. However, one of the scars didn't heal correctly and left me with a constant throbbing pain for nearly two years. Looking at me from the outside you would have never known. A shirt always covered that part of my skin, and I looked healthy and fit. But you might have wondered why I always kept my right shoulder back and never gave a full hug.

What felt to my friends like a warm embrace was actually very painful to me, because it touched the spot where my scar was throbbing and raw. I would jerk back, withdraw, and hug only from the side, and they might have wondered why.

"I wonder why he doesn't really give me a hug," they must have thought back then. In an effort to understand, they might have come up with theories of their own. "Maybe he doesn't like me." "Maybe he is self-centered." "Maybe he is deceptive and hiding something from me."

They probably wouldn't have guessed that a warm hug was actually a rather painful experience for me. They didn't cause the pain; it was from another source. But they could unknowingly activate it when they touched the painful spot, and so I withdrew in self-protection.

For a number of months I couldn't wear a seat belt normally, because the shoulder strap went directly across my scar and created constant irritation. To compensate, I wore the shoulder strap under my arm rather than over my shoulder. Suppose you were a police officer who stopped me for a routine check. "What is this guy's problem?" you might think. "Doesn't he know how to wear a seat belt? Doesn't he know that putting it under his arm is actually dangerous? If there were an accident, he could get hurt!"

My behavior wouldn't make sense to you. You might think I am irresponsible, lazy, or a rebel at heart. It probably would never occur to you that I was protecting a wound. Self-protection makes sense when you understand the nature of the wound. It does, however, create a whole host of other problems.

The same protection that keeps you from pain also blocks out all kinds of good things. It can desensitize you from healthy things you need to feel. While you experience yourself inside as soft and vulnerable, others can experience you as cold and hard.

Of course, it would be best if the wounds could be healed and the self-protection removed. If you are feeling impatient, stay with me—we will come back to this later. But for now we still need to look on to the fourth father gift: the gift of place.

Place

Admittedly, this is the hardest gift to understand. It helps to think about some of your core desires that are actually expressions of this need. You want your life to count, to make a difference. You want to fit in somewhere, to belong, to be noticed and missed. You want to find the spot where you can live out your calling, be who you were truly created to be. You want to be somehow unique. Nobody wants to feel as if their presence on earth is redundant, unnecessary, or forgotten. This is why the pharaohs built pyramids to be monuments to their greatness long after they died.

Fathers have a unique ability to give the gift of place to their children, an ability they rarely fully recognize. I've already told you my dad was a missionary by vocation and a farmer at heart. I also told you that he traveled a lot. He was always convinced that God hadn't made a mistake when he called him to lead a mission organization and his family. He wanted to be faithful with both of these sacred trusts.

One of the decisions he made was not to travel during the summer or during school vacations when we were at home. This was also the best time for gardening, and soon we were "borrowing" the large vacant lot next to our home to expand our production. The owner let us use it for free in exchange for keeping the weeds down, and before long the entire plot was in cultivation.

Before anything was planted, Dad took all of us out to stand on the newly upturned dirt. "I'd like to give each of you kids a piece of this garden," he announced, "to care for and to grow whatever you want. I'll help you plant it and teach you how to take care of it. The fruit that grows there is yours, and you will have the privilege of making that plot your own."

Note that he said "privilege." Dad wasn't doing this because he couldn't manage the entire garden by himself. In reality, he could manage it much easier on his own. Instead he chose this family project as a training ground for his children, a place where they could learn responsibility and stewardship, a place where they could experience what it was like to have *place*.

I chose a spot near the yard so I wouldn't have to walk as far. Then I sorted through a basket full of seed packets. After a long stretch of deliberation (remember, I was slow), I made my announcement.

I wanted to grow popcorn.

This may come as a surprise to you, but you can actually grow popcorn. I didn't know that either. As soon as I found out, that's what I wanted to do. I wanted my "place" to be different from the rest, unique. Dad helped me plant my popcorn. He taught me how to water it and how to weed. We would walk out together to inspect it and marvel at how fast the stalks of strangely colored corn were growing.

I almost regretted my decision when Joyce's tomatoes started to ripen and Steve's cucumbers began showing up on the dinner table. My popcorn was the last crop to be harvested. We didn't bring it in until late in the fall, well after the first freeze. Even then there was no popcorn to be eaten. It still had to dry to just the right moisture level so that the small bit of water at the core of the kernel would explode with the right force when the kernel was heated.

By Christmas we had popcorn. My plot of ground had been extremely fruitful. There was more popcorn than I ever imagined. I could have popcorn whenever I wanted! Of course, my favorite time to eat it was when we had company and dinner was almost finished. That's when my mom would suggest, "Hey, let's have some of Dave's popcorn." My eyes would light up. "Dave's popcorn!" Although there were lots of people in our crowded house, that didn't bother me because I had my place. This was *my* popcorn!

Remember what we learned in John chapter 5? Place brings *honor*.

I felt this honor when Dad gave me the job of packing on family vacation. "You have an eye for fitting things together," he would say. "You'll do a great job of this." When Mom would ask where to find things, Dad would turn to me. "You'll need to ask Dave; he is in charge of packing."

"In charge of packing." I liked the sound of that.

I experienced Dad's care again as a young man when I began to lead a fledgling new ministry to young people on military bases. "The ranking chaplains need to know what you are doing," he said, "because your work is really important." He somehow arranged a meeting with the Army chief of chaplains, who happened to also be a two-star general, and soon Dad and I were traveling to Washington, D.C., together. After finding our way through a labyrinth of halls in the Pentagon, we were ushered in to the general's office.

"I want you to know about my son's ministry," my dad said by way of introduction, and then he turned the conversation over to me. For some reason, I wasn't nervous. Crazy as it seems, I felt secure in my place. I could sense my father was thinking ahead, preparing things, blocking for me, opening the way. Not all fathers recognize the power of their words to affirm, strengthen, and prepare their children to do big things. Worse, they fail to see how their words can wound—sometimes for a lifetime.

Alex's dad was a gifted banker, well-known and highly respected in the community. Often late in the evening, Alex could see him in his study, surrounded by tall bookcases and important certificates hanging on the wall. He wanted to be near him, to feel the respect that came from his dad's strength and achievement. He slipped through the door quietly and stood there, wordlessly watching.

"What do you want?" his dad asked brusquely, momentarily looking up from his work.

"I don't know," Alex replied shyly, sitting down on an empty chair beside the door.

His dad continued to write, then glanced up to see Alex following his every move.

"If you don't want anything, what are you doing here? You're interrupting me. Get out," he said. His carelessly spoken, harsh words wounded his son deeply. Alex fought back the tears as he slipped off the chair and closed the office door. The pain was searing and sharp. He tried to control it, stuff it down inside where it didn't show. "Why is there no place for me in my father's world?" he thought as he tried to swallow his pain.

That wasn't the only time he experienced a father wound. On numerous occasions over the following years, Alex was on the receiving end of his father's gruff treatment and lack of affirmation.

If one of the signs of a father wound is self-protection, the other manifestation is distortion, something I refer to as the "amplifier." The hurt and the wound that have been pushed down don't go away. Later on this pain finds its way out by coloring similar situations in the future. For example, a closed door feels like total rejection. A look away is magnified and creates a feeling of utter

abandonment. Our response doesn't match the event that just occurred, which is why we overreact. We think we hear a message
being told to us in the present, but it is actually coming to us from
the past.

As a grown man, Alex was leading a fruitful and innovative
ministry, one with national impact. Yet he constantly felt threatened, as if everyone around him wanted to take it from him. He
drove others and himself to the point of exhaustion, trying to prove
he was something to somebody. Everyone respected his ministry, so
why this constant need to defend or prove?

It only took a bit of criticism and Alex would lash out like
he was protecting his very life. He was losing his team, losing his
health. His dad wasn't alive anymore, yet he was still present in the
lurking pain that distorted Alex's world, driving him to respond as
if he were in constant danger of losing his place.

By God's grace, there was an answer for Alex, and there's one
for me and you.

We'll get there; I promise.

But for now we need to stop and reflect on what we've seen.
Let's look again at the words I wrote on my paper at the end of the
last chapter: *All of us have been marked by what we experienced from our
fathers. This imprint shapes us long after we have left the home. Where we have
received **father gifts**, we will find healthy **giving** and **receiving**. Where
we experienced **father vacuums**, we will find **deadness** (the corpse)
and **pulls** (the vacuum cleaner).*

Now we can add this:

*Where we have experienced **father wounds**, we will find **self-
protection** (armor) and **distortion** (the amplifier).*

Make sure you catch these symptoms—they are important.

But where do we find healing?

Symptoms

Inside	Outside
Gifts	Giving → Receiving ←
Vacuums —	Deadness Pulls
Wounds	Self-Protection Distortion

6

FATHER MAPPING

If you are anything like me, reading stories about fathers stirs up lots of memories and emotions. In your journey through these last pages, you may have remembered special times with your own dad, or felt the ache of loss as you realize he wasn't there for you. There may have been some jabs of pain as your heart went out to Martin, Daniel, or Alex, and strong emotion as you felt some of your own wounds resonate with theirs.

If you are a mother, you may be thinking of your own children and hoping your husband will read this. You see your kids longing for something from their father and sense he is a bit confused about exactly what they need.

If you are a dad like me, you may be wondering what your kids would say about you if they read this book. "How am I doing as a dad?" you think. "I don't want to fail."

Perhaps other faces are coming to mind as you read, people you care about who have huge father needs. You're hoping you will learn something in these pages that will equip you to help them.

Or maybe you are reading with detachment, perhaps a bit of skepticism. For now you're gathering information, trying to understand. You'd like to treat this as an interesting study, a place to expand your knowledge. Just don't get too personal.

If any of these descriptions fits you, there is something you need to know.

You are at a crossroad.

Up till now I have led you through my early process of discovery. I've told you why I first started studying the fatherhood of God and what I initially learned. However, I can't explain the rest of this story in such a linear way. My study of the fatherhood of God stretched another ten years and took so many twists and turns that I honestly can't retrace my steps. But that's probably good. We need to leave my story now and switch to a different one.

Yours.

There are scores of books dealing with father issues and many on the fatherhood of God. I have read stacks of them. But none of that information does much good unless it brings a real and lasting transformation in your life. My goal is for you to experience the redemption, restoration, and riches God has prepared for you. That won't happen unless you go from a passive observer to an active participant. What we will cover in the rest of this book could radically change your life.

Or make no difference at all.

It all depends on what you do from this point forward.

So if you are thinking about your husband, let that go for now. If you are wondering how to help a friend, put that aside for a bit. Fathers, I don't even want you to start by trying to be a better dad to your kids. The best thing you can do for them right now is to start with your own heart. If you need to understand everything before you begin, give it up. Take a risk. What do you have to lose?

If you are like me, you need a deeper connection with the father heart of God.

For this to happen, you have to start doing some work of your own as you read. You'll need to stop along the way and complete some assignments. You'll have to be brutally honest. You'll need courage to press through your own inner resistance and fear. You'll need faith to believe what God says in his Word is true.

I'll tell you right now where we are headed. There are three main steps in the process of healing. You won't go through these just once in life. God will take parts of you through the process of redemption and then double back again to redeem something new. Once that's finished, he'll start again and bless you with something more, if you're willing. But at some point the process of father redemption needs to begin. Here are the three main steps:

Awareness – Cleansing – Restoration

Before you know what needs to be redeemed, or even know what could be restored, you need an accurate read on your present state. You need awareness.

When you visit a doctor, even for a routine physical, he or she always starts by assessing your current condition. A nurse will ask you a long list of routine questions, and your vital signs will be taken. Then the doctor will follow up with a more in-depth examination. Medical professionals know it is reckless to begin treatment without a proper diagnosis, and impossible to diagnose without a thorough exam. As one of my Bible college professors said: "Too many people are fed before they are hungry, they are clothed before they know they are naked."

So before we go any further, I am asking you to follow God into the examination room. We need to take a look at your heart. I'm a visual person, so to help me stay on track I use a simple diagram. You saw it at the end of chapter 3.

The reason why these four father gifts are so profound is that they fill four basic needs in your heart. Just like your physical heart pumps life and sustenance to the rest of the body, so these four gifts provide your soul the resources it needs to bring life to both you and others. These four needs are right at the core of your being and present in every person on this earth.

Your physical heart also has four chambers, each designed to both give and receive blood. In these chambers a powerful flow is energized, as the life-giving blood is gathered from the lungs and veins and then pumped out to the rest of your body.

In the same way, when you are receiving the father gifts of identity, love, pleasure, and place, you will be capable of bringing these resources to your activities, to your work, to your family, and to everyone around you. These deep needs can only be truly filled through a connection to the fatherhood of God. Yet our examination needs to start with a look at your earthly father, since he was the one who made that father "imprint" on your heart when it was pliable and being formed. This imprint still affects you today.

If we could perform a soul-level "X-ray" of your heart, we would see three things in these four heart chambers. We would find *father gifts*, *father wounds*, and *father vacuums*. Since the "X-ray" can be a bit grainy and hard to read, you can gather important clues about what is happening inside by observing your behavior on the outside. Do you remember the way each of these three realities expresses itself? By way of a quick review, here they are:

Father gifts – healthy giving and receiving

Father vacuums – deadness and pulls (the corpse and the vacuum cleaner)

Father wounds – self-protection and distortion (armor and the amplifier)

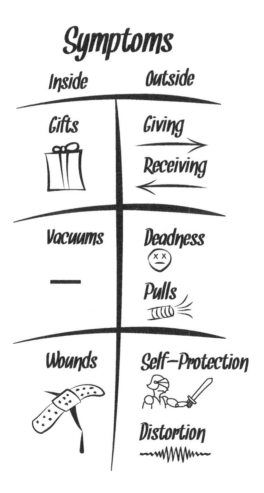

When I'm sitting with someone one-on-one, I usually take out a piece of paper and draw a diagram showing the four key areas of their heart. Then I have them color in the portion they think is filled with gifts, wounds, or vacuums. This serves as a visual "diagnostic" for us as we move forward with the next steps. But since you are evaluating your heart on your own, the two short questionnaires below may be better at providing a diagnosis. The result will help you quickly assess what you have received from your dad, as well as the current condition of those areas today.

Imprint Questionnaire

Start by considering the "imprint" your earthly father has made on your life in these four key heart areas—identity, love, pleasure, and place. With "10" as the total, your goal is to quantify the degree your father's words and actions have left you with a gift, wounded you, or created a vacuum in your heart. This is not a scientific measurement but more of an intuitive call based on what you have read so far in this book.

Take, for example, your identity. Your father's words and actions may have given you an overall feeling of great worth—which is a gift, so you might give that a "5." He was attentive, made time to talk and play with you, and always showed up at key events like games or special performances. This made you feel important and valuable to him. And yet he might still have wounded you by criticizing not just your actions but your very identity, calling you "clumsy" or "stupid" or making fun of you at times. Though you laughed it off, those words actually went deep, so you might give the category of wounds a "3." Then, if you feel a vacuum because your dad rarely affirmed your particular gifts and abilities, or said anything to you that helped you understand how God had uniquely made you, you might give that category a "2."

That said, your chart would look like this:

EXAMPLE (total = 10)

	Gifts	Wounds	Vacuum
Identity	5	3	2

You may find it helpful to ask, "What **gifts** have I received from my dad in the area of defining my identity? In what ways might my father have **wounded** me in establishing my personal identity? How might his negligence or lack of leadership have created a **vacuum** in my identity?" As you fill out the chart below, ask similar questions regarding his impact on your experience of love, pleasure, and place.

Your Imprint

	Gifts	Wounds	Vacuum
Identity			
Love			
Pleasure			
Place			

Now, draw a circle around the area with the lowest "gifts" score. What do you notice as you look at the results? Is there a new insight you were unaware of?

For instance, let's say the gift of love ranked the lowest for you. In that case, consider how the wounds and father vacuums caused by your dad may, in turn, be influencing your ability to truly enter into the unconditional love that your heavenly Father has for you today. In other words, if your dad never said those three words that we all long to hear from our fathers—namely, "I love you"—it's entirely possible you struggle to believe it when your heavenly Father says he loves you with an unconditional love.

To be sure, some have experienced such healing as they've entered into the transforming power of Jesus that they have been "re-fathered" by God. They are able to receive his identity, embrace his love, feel his pleasure, and know their place in spite of what they experienced at home. But often the wounds and vacuums created by an earthly father make it difficult for a person to freely enjoy all the riches offered in a relationship with their heavenly Dad.

Your father needs are much deeper than your dad can provide—after all, even the best earthly fathers are incomplete. So don't take it as a criticism of your dad if you recognize that there is still a vacuum in a given area. You are not giving your dad a grade right now, but looking at the current state of your heart.

Symptoms Questionnaire

While the Imprint Questionnaire helps you look back at your childhood and the shaping made by your earthy father, the Symptoms Questionnaire focuses on the present and what you are currently experiencing in these four key areas. Read the overall category definition and then work through the symptoms, evaluating on a scale of 1–5 if they are either "not true at all" or "very true" about you.

1. **Identity** – John 5:16–19

Who am I? Am I valuable? Do I have to be just like you to be significant? Am I competent? Capable?

Without identity from the Father you will be defined by the people and circumstances around you. This will be constantly changing and unstable. You will be very vulnerable to your environment and not have a clear sense of self.

	Not true at all				Very true
Identity	1	2	3	4	5
I feel like a failure.					
I often compare myself to others.					
Sometimes I hate myself.					
I don't like my body.					
I'm not happy with the personality God gave me.					
I don't like the gifts and abilities God gave me.					
I don't feel that who I am has much worth or value.					
I am much more aware of my weaknesses than my strengths.					
I often feel that if others found out who I really am they would reject me.					
I often find myself putting on masks so I can be acceptable and fit in with others around me.					
Total					

2. **Love** – John 5:20

Am I loved unconditionally? Am I precious and treasured to someone? Do I matter to anyone? Does someone care deeply about me? Do I feel and hear your love and affection?

Without love from the Father you will be constantly trying to gain love from those near you. Their love will never be enough, and you will be chronically disappointed. You may cope by turning off your emotions and becoming distant and cold.

Love	Not true at all				Very true
	1	2	3	4	5
I am one of those people who doesn't need love.					
When people express love to me it never seems to be enough to really satisfy me.					
I have a basic mistrust of others and feel it is only a matter of time before they disappoint me.					
Others say they don't feel loved by me.					
I know in my mind that God loves me, but I don't feel it.					
It is hard for me to express love to others.					
I feel awkward, nervous, and vulnerable in situations where affection is given or expected.					
Others experience me as cold and emotionless.					
I rarely feel totally safe in relationships with others.					
I can be easily manipulated by someone who expresses love and affection toward me.					
Total					

3. **Pleasure** – John 5:30, 41–44

Are you proud of me? Do you delight in me? Are you pleased with who I am? Do you enjoy my presence? Do you like being with me? Do I bring you joy?

Without pleasure from the Father you will become addicted to pleasing people and vulnerable to hedonism. You may cope by avoiding all possibility of failure or rejection.

Pleasure	Not true at all				Very true
	1	2	3	4	5
I'm constantly looking for approval from those around me.					
If someone is disappointed in me I feel devastated.					
I have a hard time taking risks because I am afraid of failure.					
I often replay the past and regret the things I didn't do well.					
I am constantly preparing myself for others to be disappointed in me—even when they are not.					
I often feel discouraged and unmotivated.					
Sometimes I feel I can't do anything right.					
I am often thinking of what can make me feel better and am drawn to whatever will boost my emotions—even if is not good for me (food, alcohol, pornography, unhealthy relationships, medication).					
I feel passionless, without excitement, dead to joy and healthy pleasure.					
I rarely feel that God is pleased with me or that he delights in me.					
Total					

4. **Place** – John 5:21–27

Do I have purpose? Does my life matter? Is there some place that is uniquely mine? Do I fit? Do I belong? Am I a part of something bigger than myself? Do I have something to give? Would you notice if I were gone?

Without place from the Father you will be constantly fighting to make a place for yourself. You will fear that your life has no significance and be easily threatened by others. You may cope by scaling back your expectations, making a place that is small but defensible—like when people curl up in a ball, hide behind something, or retreat to a corner.

	Not true at all				Very true
Place	1	2	3	4	5
I feel threatened when I am around someone who is secure and successful.					
I don't feel confident in my role at home.					
I don't feel fulfilled in my place at school or work.					
I am looking for direction and purpose in life—and haven't been able to find it.					
When someone criticizes me I overreact and feel they are trying to take something from me.					
I sometimes use power plays of anger, aggression, or demand to defend my place.					
I feel a constant need to prove myself.					
I often feel insecure and shrink back from my God-given responsibilities.					

I feel restless and easily distracted by "greener grass" somewhere different from where I am.					
It is hard for me to feel satisfied with my lot in life.					
Total					

Now look back over the big picture of what you discovered. Do you see any patterns? Since these four areas represent foundational needs of your soul, father deficiencies will have a broad and profound impact on your life. You may have so learned to live in your current reality that you never even considered it could change, much like a person with a chronic allergy cannot imagine living without a runny nose.

On the other hand, you may simply believe the passage of time will bring relief. But, much like a patient with heart disease, time will generally cause other complications to develop, as your condition becomes more and more entrenched. Deficiencies, over time, tend to damage.

Would you like to experience true, lasting, supernatural change? Through the work of the Father, Son, and Holy Spirit, and the power of God's Word, the symptoms you identified above can be addressed and the health of your soul restored. It will be a challenging process, but it's absolutely worth it. Are you ready?

7

SEEKING THE SOURCE

I'd like to let you in on a secret, one you may have already guessed: you will never get everything you need from your earthly father.

You might want to read that again. *You will never get everything you need from your earthly father.* He is flawed, imperfect, and deeply impacted by father issues of his own. In fact, I don't believe he was ever designed to meet all your father needs. Why? Because your dad is not the source of fatherhood, just a steward of it. His role was to create categories and provide experiences that would later allow you to fully connect with the fatherhood of God. Look at what Paul says in Ephesians 3:14–15: "For this reason I kneel before the Father, from whom every family in heaven and on earth derives its name."

In my Bible there is a footnote attached to the word "family," with an explanation of what it actually means. In the original Greek, this word is *fatherhood*. It would sound awkward if we used this word, but what Paul really meant is this: "For this reason I kneel before the Father (*pater*), from whom all fatherhood (*patria*) in heaven and earth derives its name."

Your dad's fatherhood is not sourced in itself but stewarded from another higher power—namely, God the Father. It is a small derivative of a profoundly greater and richer fatherhood: the fatherhood of God. This FATHERHOOD gives definition ("name") to all family relationships in the universe. Restoring our proper connection to the fatherhood of God is a much greater theme in Scripture than most of us realize.

Usually we first come to know God personally in the person of Jesus. He is our Savior, God made flesh, and so it is only natural that we experience an immediate connection to him. After that comes the adventure of learning to know the Holy Spirit. He is a bit more mysterious, but his indwelling voice and much-needed power begin to intrude on us in many ways throughout the day. The apostle John put it this way: "But the Advocate, the Holy Spirit, whom the Father will send in my name, will teach you all things and will remind you of everything I have said to you" (John 14:26). The "Advocate" (or the "Counselor") becomes more known and distinct as we recognize his voice and appreciate his wisdom.

Of course, we often refer to "God" in general, but usually what we have in mind when we speak this word is the Godhead, the Trinity, all three of them together. Naturally it is important to know the Three in One, since God's oneness is unique and particularly emphasized in Scripture through passages like the Shema, a Jewish prayer that starts in Deuteronomy 6:4: "Hear, O Israel: The LORD our God, the LORD is one."

But what about God the Father? What about the member of the Trinity who describes himself to us with this unique and meaning-filled title? Do we have a personal relationship with him? One of the first verses I memorized as a young boy was John 14:6: "Jesus answered, 'I am the way and the truth and the life. No one comes to the Father except through me.'"

I've quoted this verse many times in the years since then, most often when I've shared the gospel. I've said things like, "Jesus is the way, the truth, the life! This is profound and wonderful news!" or "Jesus is the way to salvation! He is the way to have your sins forgiven, the only way to become a Christian. He is the way to heaven, the way to eternal life. No one can get there, except through him!"

All these statements are true. But they are not what this verse is saying. Look at it again. Where is the "way" designed to take us? To the Father. "No one comes to the *Father* except through me" (emphasis added).

Don't miss this. I am saved, so I can know the Father; my sins are forgiven, so I can be with him. Heaven is a great place because he is there, and becoming a Christian is something to look forward to because it means joining his family. Our destination is the Father; all these other benefits only have meaning in relationship to him.

Are we making it through salvation, through forgiveness, through Jesus all the way to the Father? Or are we stopping somewhere along the way? This should be obvious, right? Jesus came to make the Father known. So why did Philip, just two verses after John 14:6, say this: "Lord, show us the Father and that will be enough for us"?

Philip had been with Jesus for at least two years, listening to his teaching and watching his life. Right before Philip's statement Jesus had said, "If you really know me, you will know my Father as well" (John 14:7). And now this request! How could Philip be so dense? How could he know so much about Jesus and still not know the Father? "Don't you know me, Philip," Jesus answered, "even after I have been among you such a long time? Anyone who has seen me has seen the Father. How can you say, 'Show us the Father'?" (John 14:9).

I don't know for sure, but I think after Jesus said this Philip was still confused. Just like many of us, he was not seeing *through* Jesus *to* the Father. In spite of all the time he had spent with Jesus, he didn't fully know him. He didn't realize one of Jesus' prime objectives was (and is) to reveal the Father to us.

So . . . now you know.

Look what happens if you go back to your father map and insert God the Father into every one of your heart chambers. Your problems will be solved. Your needs will be fully met in his limitless fatherhood. Your sense of identity, love, pleasure, and place will be restored. Right?

Absolutely right.

Philip was essentially saying, "Show us the Father and we will be *satisfied*." All those father needs we have been talking about can be fully satisfied in him.

From the outside, Don had it all—a great career, a beautiful wife named Naomi, and two precious kids. As CEO of a $10 billion energy firm in Texas, Don enjoyed the benefits of power and financial success. It seemed everything he touched turned to gold.

Three years later he was living alone in a rented apartment, halfway across the country. Outer success had increased the pressure on the emptiness he experienced inside and the lack of health in his key relationships. Fed up with the charade, his wife had divorced him and had taken the kids.

Then the sale of his company forced him out of his job. Far from God, he was crumbling in on himself, finding that while his job skills were well-honed, his soul didn't have a foundation. He was harsh and demanding in relationships, self-centered and proud.

When I met Don ten years later, I wouldn't have guessed any of this rough sailing had happened. I could see in an instant how much Don adored his wife and children, and I personally experienced his fatherly interest and love directed toward me. Watching him relate to others, I sensed a fatherly care that seemed to pour out from him toward everyone around him.

Blessed with a deep walk with God, he was again serving in a key business role, but with the relaxed spirit of someone who had nothing to prove. He was married again—to Naomi! I couldn't believe it was his second marriage to his first wife or that these two kids were the same ones who had been taken from him. "What happened?" I asked.

"God took me to the end of my rope—and then drew me to himself," he answered. "Then I met God the Father and," his eyes became moist as he talked, "I fell so in love with the Father that I didn't want to do anything but spend time in his presence. I lost desire for anything else but him. All of those hours with the Father—they healed my soul."

I could tell he meant every word.

"Really?" you might be saying. "I mean, that all sounds nice, but . . . wow. Somehow I can't picture that working for me."

I told you earlier about my father vacuum in the area of love. Remember the "shock treatment" I received when my girlfriend, Connie, dumped me? Remember the steps forward I had taken when I purposefully chose to open up and learn to love her? I had made good progress.

That is why it bothered me to hear these words.

"God really loves you, Dave!" a friend told me after a staff meeting.

"Uh-huh, I guess so," I responded, shrugging my shoulders.

"Look at all the ways he is taking care of you. He really must love you."

"Wow, uh, right," I mumbled, obviously unaffected.

Laurie stopped and fixed me with a penetrating stare.

"That doesn't mean anything to you, does it?"

"Well, uh, you know . . ." I stammered.

"Dave, that didn't mean anything to you at all, did it?" she continued, obviously disturbed.

I felt caught. No, it didn't mean anything to me. Those words had rolled off me like water rolling off the back of a duck. I knew

God loved me, so why didn't it penetrate? Why didn't it make a difference?

I couldn't understand it. God the Father is rich and generous; I was poor and needy. I knew I needed his father love. But if he was offering exactly what I was longing for, why didn't his love penetrate my heart and satisfy my soul?

I needed to know the answer to that question.

So do you.

8

DEFINING MOMENTS

I hope you completed the father mapping. What you discovered there is essential for making this more than an interesting exercise in understanding. Your personal participation is crucial for what lies ahead. I believe the fact that you picked up this book and made it this far isn't an accident.

Your Father is very active in his pursuit of you. You are on this journey by design—his design. You are unique and different from every other person in the world, and he knows that. The way he reaches out to you is tailor-made to who you are, and because of that, distinct from all his other relationships.

Because his character and purpose is always the same, you will find parts of yourself in each of these stories I am telling. But he is most interested in *your* story, the one that is being told right now as you read this, the one your Father knows every detail of, from the very beginning.

He wants to meet you in your story, and that is why it is so important for you to let him intrude on whatever else is going on in your life right now. You need to give him your full attention. This is his time for you, because his sovereignty has led you, right now, to these very pages.

He is leading you to himself. *Will you follow*

So if you haven't finished the father map, go back right now and complete it before we continue. I ask you on his behalf!

As we discovered in the last chapter, the Father is the only One who can fully meet your needs for identity, love, pleasure, and place. This is good news!

But sometimes this good news can feel like a mockery to us. We know it from Scripture (see Psalm 63:1–5), so we believe—in theory. But it doesn't quite seem to match our experience. Why don't the Father's resources reach the places where we are needy? Why don't they penetrate and fill us till we are "satisfied"?

Remember the three steps to healing? Here they are again:

Awareness – Cleansing – Restoration

The second step, *cleansing*, is crucially important. If you try to go directly from *awareness* to *restoration*, you will run into a barrier. This is because what looks like an empty chamber of your heart is actually not empty; it has been filled with other things.

If an artery is blocked with a clot, the good blood doesn't flow, even though the heart is pumping for all its worth.

A milk carton half-filled with spoiled milk can't be made nourishing for breakfast by pouring in good milk on top. First you have to cleanse the container of the spoiled substance, then there is space for the liquid that is good.

Many people are frustrated on the path to restoration because they skip this essential step of cleansing. Without it, their efforts at restoration don't bring the change they hoped for, and in turn, they are disillusioned. There is no shortcut. You can't be filled by the Father without being emptied of whatever has already taken his place. You can't experience the flow of God's father heart without removing the barriers that stand in his way.

Remember how we did a soul-level "X-ray" to discover the imprint your earthly father left on your heart? Now we need to do a spirit-level "ultrasound" to find out what you have done with what you received. You won't be able to do this all at once. You'll need the help of the Holy Spirit, the Counselor, to show you the way.

First of all, stop reading for a moment. Close your eyes and pray. In your mind, scan the four chambers of your heart you explored in the father mapping exercise. In this next section you will need to concentrate on just one of them. Ask the Spirit to show you which one it is. Then listen. He will speak to you by directing your mind or activating your memories, tugging a certain direction on your heart, and bringing specific Scriptures to your mind. Keep listening. When you have clear guidance from him, put your finger on one of the four father gifts below, the one he wants you to concentrate on right now.

Identity / Love / Pleasure / Place

Don't second-guess the Spirit's leading. Keep your finger there a moment and let that category settle into your mind. You'll need to focus on that gift right now and leave the others for later.

Look at that word again. Reflect on why the Spirit is taking you to that particular gift at this time. Why is it so important for you? He may remind you of ways this need is expressing itself in your current relationships, or show you signs of deadness, pulls, self-protection, or distortion. Let him stir up all the information that is important to him.

Now let's make this more specific. In each of these four areas there are certain defining moments—memories or events that have particular significance to you. Sometimes they are important because of things that were said or the pain you experienced, like the day Martin found out his father was no longer coming home.

Other times these defining moments are important because they symbolize a repeating pattern that left a permanent mark on you. Alex's memory of the exchange in his father's office is an example of this. For someone else that might have been a quick encounter to be brushed off and forgotten, but for Alex it put words and emotion to a pattern he had experienced over and over from his dad, one that repeated many times over the years that followed. Because of this, Alex's memory of the event was loaded with deep symbolic meaning and full of emotion.

Sometimes our fathers are not even a part of these defining moments. What is significant in these memories is not his *presence* but his *absence*. In our moment of need there was no clear communication of identity, love, pleasure, or place from a father voice. Without that, we were adrift and "fatherless."

You may be thinking right now, "Hey, I had a mother too, and she was pretty important to me! What about her?"

You are absolutely right. Your mom is hugely significant, and we will talk more about her role later on, but we need to leave that for later. Right now I want you to stay focused on your father needs and how they have impacted you.

So how do you discover those defining moments?

Again, it is a good thing we have an expert Counselor to help us. The Holy Spirit works inside you to "guide you into all the truth" (John 16:13–15). He does not speak words of his own but reveals to you things from the Father. He knows which of these defining moments are important for you to remember, and he will bring them to mind. Trust him.

Let me illustrate what I mean by this.

I always enjoyed the time I got to spend with my friend Brian but usually left a bit confused. Brian was a successful financial manager, community leader, and elder at his church. Extremely competent in work, he also cared deeply for people. I'd asked him to help advise us on organizational development in our mission, and Brian had so much to offer. Yet when we talked, it felt like a switch was going on and off, like the door would open and then quickly close. I would experience this wonderful engagement with Brian for a bit, and then he would disappear, disconnect. He would look me intently in the eye for a while, and then he would suddenly stare off into a corner as if I were no longer there. Our conversation would be lively and engaging, and then abruptly stop as if he had mentally left the room. It was confusing, and I often left wondering if I had done something wrong.

Then a family crisis started to spin his world. His unwed daughter came home with the news she was pregnant, then lost the baby and spiraled into depression. Rather than engaging, Brian withdrew in fear, unable to lead his family and father his hurting daughter. She needed father care, but Brian was locked up and didn't know what to do. Torn between his own sense of failure and the sorrow he felt for his daughter, Brian couldn't move toward her with engagement and strength.

I offered to jump in with him, and we met again—this time to talk about his family. Trying to get some background, I asked about his father and learned Brian had lost his dad when he was twenty months old. His mom remarried, but he never emotionally connected with his stepdad, never experienced him as a father. His stepdad was more like his mom's new husband than his dad, which made him feel far from her as well.

Brian was an outstanding athlete and excelled in school. Yet he never remembers his stepdad visiting a game and never heard words of praise from him for his academic accomplishments—all of which left deep father wounds. Whenever Brian would reflect on the dad he lost, the ache seemed almost too great to bear. Like

Brian, his real dad was an athlete and would have immediately connected with Brian's love for baseball. His dad had been a man of God and a top leader in various student ministries. Brian was sure his dad would have valued his drive for excellence and championed his love for the Lord. But this wonderful father was gone, and Brian's sense of loss was overwhelming.

Now Brian was fifty-four years old, with a family of his own, but he still felt fatherless. When situations called for him to reach inside and draw on those father resources to give to others, he looked inside and saw emptiness. "I don't have it," he thought, "because I never received it." He was experiencing a father vacuum but didn't realize it at the time.

In spite of his strong reputation and success, Brian always felt other people would suddenly discover the truth and find out that in spite of what he could accomplish, inside there was a vacuum.

As he shared his story, my experience of him began to make sense. Engagement, and then sudden disengagement. A flow of his heart, and then nothing, like the door would open briefly and then slam shut. I wondered how this was impacting his daughter.

"Brian, we have to go to the Counselor right now," I said, moved by what I had heard. "The needs you had for a father are real needs, and you still have them today. Without these needs met, you won't have the resources to give to others, and your daughter needs them from you right now. But in order to open those channels, you will need to do some cleansing."

I explained the nature of defining moments, how these key events are full of meaning that helps us unlock the present through specific steps of healing. We bowed our heads, and both of us prayed that the Holy Spirit would bring these defining moments to his mind. The prayer ended, and I prepared myself to listen, only to be interrupted by a slap on the shoulder as Brian said, "Well, I sure am curious how God is going to answer this prayer. Hey, are we about finished?" He began to reach for his coat.

I started to laugh. "Brian, we just prayed for the Holy Spirit to speak to you, and you are not even going to listen!" I said incredulously. "That's like asking a question and then not waiting for the answer."

"You mean, you think he is going to answer right now?" Brian replied.

"Of course I do," I said. "We asked in Jesus' name. Jesus said that whatever we asked in his name, according to his will, would be given to us. Don't you think it is his will that you come to know his Father in a deeper way? Don't you think he would want to communicate to you through his Spirit, since his Spirit was sent to lead us into 'all the truth' and be our Counselor and guide? If you asked me a question, and I wanted you to know the answer, why would I wait two weeks to give it to you?" I answered.

"Well, okay, I guess we could pray again. I really don't have to be anywhere else right now," he said reluctantly, settling back into his chair.

We prayed to the Father again, asking him to show Brian the key memories he needed to recall. This time it was quiet as we created space to listen. The Spirit was speaking to me as we waited, highlighting key parts of the stories I had already heard. When Brian opened his eyes, I asked him what the Spirit had brought to his mind.

"Well, I don't know if it was me or the Spirit," he said, full of doubt.

"Let's trust him," I replied, "and get it out there. If it is not from him, it will become clear."

"Okay," he said slowly, "but I really don't see how this relates to the situation with my daughter."

I could tell he was feeling uncomfortably vulnerable. It would be tough to walk back through painful memories and confront his loss full in the face. But I also knew this path would bring him great blessing, if he had the courage to walk it.

"Brian, what do you have to lose?" I said. "What is the worst thing that can happen? What if we seek God for a couple of hours and it doesn't make any difference? At the very least you will be rewarded for seeking, because Hebrews 11:6 promises God 'rewards those who earnestly seek him.' Even if nothing comes from your faith, God will be pleased and honored that you acted in faith, because faith always pleases him."

I could see him warming to the idea of seeking God's leading in faith.

I pressed on. "So, what is the worst outcome? You spend time and energy seeking God. Nothing changes, but he is pleased and he rewards you. That is not bad for a worst-case scenario."

"And the best case?" Brian asked, guessing where I was headed.

"The best case is that the Counselor knows what he is doing and arranged this conversation you and I are having today; that he knows dealing with your past will lead to freedom in the present and making progress on your father issues is key to giving your daughter what she needs. What do you have to lose?" I said, looking Brian in the eye, hoping his faith was stronger than his fear.

"All right," he said, taking a deep breath. "I'm ready."

In the next several minutes he replayed for me four defining moments that the Holy Spirit had brought to mind. One was in his living room at two and a half years of age, shortly after his father's death. The next occurred when his family moved and he was uprooted from his supportive community. The third was a baseball game when there was no one to watch him. And the fourth was when he left home for college. It was clear all these moments were full of potent emotion and deep meaning. But what exactly were we supposed to do with them?

We will come back to Brian's story soon, but I don't want to get ahead of your story. You have chosen one of the four father gifts to concentrate on. What are the key defining moments in this area for you? Go back to that father gift you put your finger on. Close your eyes and pray to your heavenly Father; ask him to lead you through his Holy Spirit. Ask him to bring the key defining moments to mind, the ones related to this particular father gift.

Then allow your thoughts to move back in time, like you are rewinding the tape of your life in fast motion. Let the Spirit "freeze-frame" the tape at the spots where you need to stop and take note. Roll the tape all the way back and then forward again to check and see if you caught all the places he was noting.

It will be helpful if you have at least one, and not more than four or five, of these key events. You may be confused when the tape stops, and you may wonder how this particular memory can have any significance. Don't evaluate right now; just take note of the key moments the Holy Spirit brings to mind. These may be wonderful memories that need to be underlined. But there may be scenes you don't want to see. They may be too painful, too toxic. You would rather ignore them, block them out, or will them to go away. But if the Spirit is bringing them to your mind, his intent is not to harm you in any way but to heal you and bless you. Trust him and follow his lead.

Don't proceed with this assignment without the Spirit's guidance. Make sure you file these defining moments firmly in your mind—you will need them. To ensure they are not lost, I encourage you to write a few notes to remind you of them.

You may be thinking, "Why do I have to remember these defining moments at all?" Remember the phrase "A picture is worth a thousand words"? You may want to approach your father needs in a logical, black-and-white, cognitive manner, but you experience them in living color, with all your being (mind, will, and emotions) in the richness of real life. For you to untangle your present condition properly, you need all that color, the full bandwidth in which your patterns were laid down—whether good or bad.

Once you have identified these defining moments, you need to discover where to start the cleansing process. Again, the Counselor knows that best. Stop and pray. Ask the Holy Spirit to put his finger on the particular defining moment where he wants you to begin. Remember that his leading will not be long and labored. Don't get off track doubting, wondering, or second-guessing. Affirm in prayer that Jesus is Lord of your life, submit your thoughts to him, and then trust what you are receiving from his Spirit.

Write down the defining moment where he wants you to start.

As Brian and I prayed, it was clear we needed to start with the first memory the Spirit had brought to mind, the one when he was just two and a half years old and in the living room. I began to ask him questions so I could understand this event better.

"How long was this after your father's death?" I asked. "Why do you remember the living room—what is significant about this place? What about the rest of your family? Were any of them involved? What actually happened? What was said? What was going through your head as it all unfolded? What did you feel? How did you respond? What did you think about yourself or others because of what took place there? How did that mark you or change you?"

I told Brian I wanted to understand this memory as much as possible because there was a very good reason the Spirit brought it to his mind.

Since I can't personally ask you those same questions, I'd like to ask them from this page. Can you try to put yourself back in the middle of the defining moment the Spirit brought to your mind and see and feel the specifics again? It might help you to relive this story with a friend or with your spouse. Then let them ask all the questions that come to their minds, and answer them as honestly as you can.

Reflect on the way this particular memory relates to the father gift you identified earlier. Do you feel wounds or vacuums in this place? What were you looking for that you didn't receive? Remember, our goal here is not to change your dad or punish you. If the Spirit brought this memory to mind, there is a very important reason.

There is something here that needs to be cleansed.

There is a clot in the arteries, or sour milk in the carton. Once that is removed, your heavenly Father can meet you in this very place and supernaturally provide the father gifts you need.

But before that can happen, you need to clear out some debris.

Now, put that memory on pause for a moment. In the next chapter we will learn about five common diseases of the heart and how you can constructively deal with them.

9

POISONED BY LIES

Our hearts were made to be filled up by the Father. But we live in a fallen world where sin, failure, and disappointment mark every one of the four key chambers of our hearts. This leaves debris that needs to be cleansed before those places can be renewed by him.

Some people resist looking back into the past, arguing that if Jesus has given us everything we need, we just need to believe we are new creatures and live like it. In some respects they are correct. However, the path to that goal involves another step. The Bible teaches us that the process of sanctification (becoming more like Christ) involves taking off the "old self" (our old ways of thinking, bad habits, and incorrect beliefs that still cling to us) and putting on the "new self" (new ways of thinking and new beliefs that reflect the truth of our new identity in Christ). This is an active, ongoing process. We are commanded to "put off" and "put on," which means there are specific actions we are expected to take (Ephesians 4:22–24; Colossians 3:9–10).

If we put on our new clothes without taking off the old, we are like a child who covers up his muddy jeans by simply pulling on a clean pair over the top of the dirty ones. While the final result might look good from the outside, the dirt has just been covered but has not been removed. And since the old pair remains closest to his skin, it will certainly not be a comfortable solution.

In my experience, there are five main heart diseases that clog up the chambers of our hearts. Sometimes we suffer from just one or two of them; sometimes all five are present. Let's take a look at an example of the first one: *lies*.

Other than occasionally reciting the words in the Lord's Prayer—"Our Father, who art in heaven"—Tina never called God her Father. In spite of growing up in a Christian home, she didn't see God this way. Tina reserved the word *father* only for her dad, who, as the only parent throughout her teenage years, was also Mr. Mom. It didn't occur to Tina to seek God for anything, and she only acknowledged him during quick prayers at mealtimes—it was her dad whom she turned to for everything.

Reflecting back on her relationship with her dad, Tina said, "I was always looking to my dad for wisdom, companionship, and validation that what I was doing was good—that I was on the right track." She added, "I'd pour my heart out to my dad, waking up extra early on Sunday mornings to sip tea and gush to him about school, friends, the occasional boy. I wanted to know exactly what he thought of the world, how to react to life's challenges, and what he thought of me. Each word he spoke was weighted and powerful."

It seemed to Tina that she and her dad were best friends, but things soon changed when he fell in love with a woman who lived in a different state. He began spending extended periods of time with her, leaving Tina alone for weeks at a stretch as he visited his newfound love. When he was gone, she felt abandoned—fatherless. His romantic relationship lasted nearly three years, and after every fight and breakup he would come home to Tina, and blame it all on her. She resisted this at first but soon began to believe it was true.

"I am a problem, a burden," she began saying to herself. "I cause others hurt and pain."

After her dad's tragic death from a heart attack during her last month of high school, Tina started to fixate on his words. "I am a problem," she kept replaying in her head. "I cause others hurt and pain." Her memories of her dad mingled with a bitterness that became a destructive force in her life. Soon she was slowly starving herself, trapped in a dangerous eating disorder.

The words of identity ringing in her head were not true, but they *felt* true because they came through a father's voice—*her* father's voice. To anyone reading this, the lie is immediately obvious, since we all know the message playing in her head is exactly opposite of what her heavenly Father would say. Still, deep down inside, Tina believed it. That belief turned the lie into a poison that began to destroy her from the inside out.

When friends urged her to go to God with her problem, she couldn't see how that would help. Expecting to hear the same words from him, she projected her dad's voice onto God as if it were his own. "What is the point of turning to God," she thought, "when he will just confirm that I am the problem, that I am the one causing others hurt and pain?"

I first understood the potency of father lies when talking with a friend, Tim, who was trapped in the depths of chronic depression. Trying to encourage him, I told him how much people loved and admired him, how gifted he was, and how I saw God blessing him in the ministry he was leading. My words were heartfelt and absolutely true. Yet I watched my encouragement bounce off him as if I were making it all up.

Trying to engage a stronger voice in the process, I asked Tim to look at himself through God's eyes. "What would God say if he were speaking to you right now?" I asked, hopeful this might take us further.

After a moment of contemplation, he answered, "Almost, but not quite."

"What?" I responded, confused. "You think my question is almost, but not quite?"

"No," Tim replied, "I'm telling you what God is saying when he looks at me: 'Almost, but not quite.'"

Now I was even more confused. I opened God's Word and showed Tim passages in Scripture that expressed God's view of him—and totally contradicted the words he had just said (Zephaniah 3:17; Romans 8:1; Ephesians 3:17–19). Still, it didn't seem to make any difference.

Finally, I asked about his dad. "Did you ever hear those words from your father?" I asked Tim.

"Oh yeah," he said, becoming animated for the first time in our conversation. "All the time." Then he began to tell me stories, defining moments, of when his father ridiculed his performance and spoke destructive words of identity deep into his heart. I winced in pain as I heard him repeat his father's mocking words. These were lies that *felt* like the truth. Though Tim might logically assent to something different, in his emotional heart these words were not lies at all. His belief made them true for him—and distorted the world around him to make it match what they were saying.

My words of encouragement sounded like this when they reached Tim's ears.

"Almost, but not quite."

We shouldn't be surprised to find that lies seem to have an energy all their own. Jesus told us we have an enemy who is the "father of lies" (John 8:44). He is also a murderer, bent on our destruction. Like a lion, he preys on us when we are weak and vulnerable, energizing lies designed to bring us down (1 Peter 5:8).

For Brian, his defining moment at age two and a half represented the fact that he truly was all alone. The lie here wasn't spoken by his dad; it was spoken by Brian himself (or by the father of lies) in the midst of a father vacuum. "You are alone," the words said. "You will always be alone. There is nothing you can do about it. Just don't let anyone know you are so alone, and maybe you can fool them."

These powerful lies were still affecting Brian over fifty years later.

Just like Brian, Tina, and Tim, you probably began to believe some dangerous lies in your defining moments. Sometimes these lies were spoken to you, and sometimes you spoke them to yourself as you tried to make sense of what was going on around you. These lies are like heart disease, creating pockets of unhealthiness that will actually repel the truth. When something is said to you that contradicts this lie, you reject it, explain it away, or ignore it altogether. These lies defend themselves, resist extraction, and distort your sense of reality. They must be cleansed for you to fully receive your Father's words of truth.

"This sounds interesting," you might be saying. "But what am I supposed to practically do? Do I just say, 'Oh, that's a lie,' and expect it to go away?"

You may be protesting inside because you have tried to talk yourself out of some lies in the past, telling yourself they were not true, and then found they didn't go away. One important secret to effective cleansing is to deal with the lie at its source. In Psalm 51:6 David said, "Behold, you delight in truth in the *inward being*, and you teach me wisdom in the *secret heart*" (ESV, emphasis added). As he sought cleansing from the sin of his failure with Bathsheba, he knew he needed truth. But David also needed it in the right place, in his *inward being* and *secret heart*.

Sometimes we know truth; we just don't know it in the right place. We know it in our cognitive, adult, rational minds, but in the spot where our key memories are stored we don't believe it at all. In our "inward being" and "secret heart" are non-rational beliefs that seem to have a life all their own. These emotional convictions were laid down in the past, but they are still very much a part of us today.

Taking truth to the point in our souls where it is most needed is like what a doctor does when delivering radiation to the exact spot where cancer is growing. In soul cleansing, the specific memory where the lie is stored is the place where the full force of truth needs to be applied.

The other secret to cleansing lies from our soul comes from the very core of the gospel. When Jesus began to travel and preach the good news that would bring in his kingdom, he summarized it in just two words. *"Repent* and *believe,"* he said (Mark 1:15, emphasis added). Why is this statement such good news? Why do these two words lie at the core of what Jesus was asking his followers to do?

To describe Christ's kingdom itself would take many more words than just two. We would need scores of pages to even attempt a short summary of the blessing and goodness Jesus brings when his lordship restores humankind and the universe to its original design. To capture the extent of his work to purchase our redemption would also take many words. We would need to find a way to describe his activity from eternity past, culminating in his unfathomable sacrifice on the cross and continuing as he prepares eternal bliss for those he has redeemed. This, however, is his work, done with boundless wisdom and at great cost. It is his responsibility, not ours. What, then, are we to do?

"Repent and believe."

That's it? Just two words? These two words must be very important.

What do they mean? *Repent* describes a change of direction, a decision to leave something and turn from it. *Believe* means to place your faith in what God has said, receiving what he offers. Both are very active, deliberate, and closely interconnected. Repentance empties your hands; faith fills them. Repentance surrenders your will; faith submits it to the lordship of Christ. Repentance agrees with God's evaluation of your situation; faith accepts his solution. Repentance acknowledges your fault; faith receives forgiveness. Repentance leaves the path of self-reliance; faith steps onto the path of obedience.

Repentance renounces; faith receives. They are two sides of the key that unlocks the kingdom, two interconnected actions that open the door to freedom.

Many of the factors that influence your life are out of your control. Outside it is cold and gloomy today as I write, but I can't tell the rain to stop falling, and I can't change the disturbing news about four mass murders I read in the news this morning. In the same way, I didn't decide where I would be born and had no part in choosing the family I grew up in.

Since so many formative things happened *to* you, it's easy to lose sight of what is fully under your control. Repentance and faith are always fully accessible to you. In these two areas you are never a victim but always an agent. No one can control your will in these two categories; no one can block your way. Here you are always free to act.

No matter what family you grew up in, what kind of father you did or didn't have, or what kinds of experiences life brought you, you can always repent and believe.

When we uncovered the lie that had convinced Brian he was alone and would always be alone, it felt like truth to him. We prayed and asked God to reveal his father presence into that same place (I will share with you more about this in later chapters), and it became clear that Brian was never alone. Then the Holy Spirit began to bring verses of truth to both of us. We started to look up and read aloud together verses like: "Though my father and mother forsake me, the LORD will receive me" (Psalm 27:10). "Who shall separate us from the love of Christ? . . . No, in all these things we are more than conquerors through him who loved us" (Romans 8:35, 37). We also read this powerful promise: "Never will I leave you; never will I forsake you" (Hebrews 13:5).

This Scripture passage brought tears to my eyes as I thought of Brian: "A father to the fatherless, a defender of widows, is God in his holy dwelling. God sets the lonely in families" (Psalm 68:5–6).

We sat silent for a moment, letting the power of these words sink in. Then I asked Brian if he would be willing to cleanse that lie with repentance and faith. At first he responded with a questioning look, not fully understanding that this was a place for repentance. Often we just think of repentance and faith in relationship to sin, not realizing it applies to other areas as well. In cleansing a lie, repentance is renouncing the lie and agreeing with God's assessment that it is false. Faith is actively receiving truth from God into that same place.

I told Brian I didn't fully understand how it works, but repentance and faith have a special power in the spiritual world. Somehow they can break the claim this lie has had on his soul.

Think of what happened when you repented and believed in Jesus. This simple act took you from darkness to light and gave you entrance into the family of God. But, as Martin Luther said in the first of his ninety-five theses, "When our Lord and Master Jesus Christ said, 'Repent,' he willed the *entire life* of believers to be one of repentance" (emphasis added). Repentance and faith are needed, not just at salvation, but all along the path of following Jesus.

Brian nodded in agreement, and together we entered into cleansing prayer. In the name of Jesus he renounced the lie he had believed for so many years, and he declared it to be false. He reviewed the truth we had just read, applied it to himself, and received it in the name of Jesus. Then he committed himself, in faith, to living according to that truth. I said a hearty "amen" as his witness.

From that moment, I never heard Brian say he was alone again.

When Tina began counseling to address her eating disorder, she had the privilege of meeting with a good friend of mine who specializes in cases just like hers. With great compassion, Michelle took her to the defining moments that had shaped her and uncovered the lies that were poisoning her soul. Leading her to renounce those lies and receive the truth, Tina was able to meet her heavenly Father and hear his words of identity and love.

"When my counselor first spoke to me about my Abba Father," Tina said later, "I immediately thought she was referring to my dad, but she was talking about God. Even though I lost the physical presence of my earthly father, she told me I wasn't fatherless. God is my Father—always watching over me, holding me, opening his arms, and desiring my eternal embrace. God knows my heart fully and completely. He is always pouring out love to me, never calling me 'a problem.' Learning about my Abba Father deeply changed my perspective of my purpose and what it means to be loved. Knowing this feeling of immense joy I have because of my relationship with the Father, I trust him more than anyone. Through my faith, I've found that the only one that can love me fully—going beyond my wildest ideas of what it means to be loved—is God, my Abba Father."

Wow, that is powerful stuff! Listening to Tina speak, we can hear the profound impact of restoration, made possible because she received God's truth and cleansed the lie. I hope you want to experience this too! If God has shown you some lies you need to cleanse with repentance and faith, you can begin right away. As you do, you'll find it especially beneficial to understand four more diseases of the heart.

10

SEDUCED BY IDOLS

Knowing Michael Jackson's humble beginnings, it is hard to comprehend the magnitude of his later fame. Born to an African-American working-class family in Gary, Indiana—not quite the musical capital of the world—he was the eighth of ten children. His mother was a devout Jehovah's Witness, and his dad worked an uninspiring job as a crane operator in a local steel mill. With only a single-level, three-room house to call their home, no one had much privacy or space.

A musician at heart, Joseph Jackson, Michael's father, also performed with an R&B band called the Falcons. Sensing raw musical talent in his sons, he began to train them at home, molding them into a music group that he called, appropriately, the Jackson Brothers.

Michael joined his siblings on stage at five years of age, and his natural talent and ability to charm an audience soon earned him the role of the group's lead vocalist. The young performers began to land better gigs, working their way up to opening for such well-known R&B artists as Gladys Knight and James Brown.

However, behind the scenes, things were not always pleasant in the Jackson family. As Joseph pushed his sons to succeed, he also became violent with them. "If you didn't do it the right way, he would tear you up, really get you,"[9] Michael recounted later in an interview with Martin Bashir, describing how Joe would sit in a chair with a belt in his hands while the brothers rehearsed. In spite of their success on stage, the Jackson children regularly experienced physical and emotional abuse at home.

Michael's sensitivity, one of the keys to his ability to connect with an audience on stage, also made him very vulnerable to his father's tirades. In spite of the fact that he had many brothers and sisters, Michael would often cry at night from loneliness. Fear of his father's disapproval worked him into such an emotional frenzy he would sometimes vomit at the sight of him.

When he was eight years old, the Jackson Brothers became the Jackson 5, with Michael firmly in the spotlight as a young prodigy and the main draw for the group. They set a chart record when their first four singles all peaked at number one on the Billboard Hot 100 charts. In 1979 he released his first solo album *Off the Wall*, followed by a second solo album in 1982, *Thriller*. Fueled by a groundbreaking music video, *Thriller* generated seven top 10 hits and went on to become the best-selling album in history.

Michael's sequined glove covered a hand that seemed to turn anything he touched into gold. In the years that followed, he won 13 Grammy awards and 26 American Music Awards, achieved 13 number one singles in the United States, and sold over *400 million albums* worldwide. He maintained a global presence in popular culture for four full decades and was recognized as the most successful entertainer of all time by the *Guinness Book of World Records*.

However, as time went on, Michael became even more well known for his strange antics and ever-changing appearance. He seemed bent on recovering a lost childhood, creating a private estate called Neverland (complete with rides and a Ferris wheel) and inviting young boys to spend time with him there. He struggled with anxiety and often needed medication to sleep at night.

Tragically, while rehearsing for a comeback concert series titled "This Is It," his mounting need for medication cost him his life.

After pressing his personal doctor for increased dosages that would allow him to sleep, Michael died of acute propofol and benzodiazepine intoxication on the night of June 25, 2009.

This news shocked the world and crashed websites and search engines as people scrambled for more details. The Wikimedia Foundation reported nearly a million visitors to Michael's biography within one hour, the most visitors in a one-hour period to view any article in Wikipedia's history.

People became transfixed on the story as they struggled to find the reason why such a successful performer would lose his life in such a tragic way. In an interview with CNN host Campbell Brown not long after Michael's death, Shmuley Boteach, an Orthodox Jewish rabbi who had been a close confidant to Michael, shared his perspective: "Michael always thought that he had ailments of the body. He always had a neck that hurt, a foot that was twisted. Really, he had an affliction of his soul. He was extremely lonely, he was extremely unhappy. He felt purposeless, he felt lethargic. . . . He was especially afraid of evasion, that perhaps his best years are behind him."

Boteach described Michael's efforts to reinvent himself, which included medicating away the pain. But in the end, Michael was hooked on more drugs than a human body could sustain. Although his death was tragic, Boteach says he believed it could have been prevented.

What's more, Boteach was convinced that "Michael lived with a profound fear of rejection." Boteach explained, "Michael told me once—and this is a heartbreaking conversation between us—'Shmuley, I promise I'm not lying to you,' he said. 'I'm not lying to you.' He said that twice. 'But everything I've done in pursuing fame, in honing my craft' to quote his words, 'was an effort to be loved because I never felt loved.' And he used to say that to me all the time."

Michael chased fame when what he really needed and longed for was to be loved. Boteach described Michael as a tortured soul who "from the earliest age did not know love because he felt that he had to perform to earn love. He lived in permanent insecurity. He was one of the most tortured souls I ever came across. . . . Michael really wanted his father's approval. And he loved his father very deeply. I know that in many interviews he spoke about anger towards his father. But when he was with me he said that he lived for his father's approval."

I'm not surprised to hear Michael longed for his father's approval. This is a universal need hardwired into each of us. Boteach added, "Michael wanted his father's love more than anything else. His father meant the world to him. And I think that one of the things he lived with more than anything else—the pain he lived with—was this constant feeling that he never quite earned his father's affection."[10]

Michael's story resonated with so many around the world because it was an amplified version of their own. Like all of us, he longed for the four father gifts of *identity*, *love*, *pleasure*, and *place*. Expecting them from his father, Joe, he received instead father wounds and father vacuums. Not wanting to leave these needs unmet, he naturally attempted to fill them through other things. "Everything I've done in pursing fame . . . ," he said, " was an effort to be loved because I never felt loved."

The adoration of the crowd became the substitute for the father gifts of *love* and *pleasure*. Then chemical medication became the antidote that would dull the pain of possible rejection. Without the father gift of *identity*, he constantly tried to remake himself, changing his facial structure and skin color, reinventing his image. Without the father gift of *place*, he tried to return to his childhood through Neverland and friendships with children, and reclaim something that was lost when he himself was a boy.

In spite of financial and personal success, these substitutes were never enough, and time just seemed to increase the hunger of his soul, leading to the "permanent insecurity" Boteach described in the "tortured soul" he observed. We see in Michael a tragic example of the second disease of the heart, one that afflicts us all. This is the disease of *idolatry*.

As John Calvin so aptly stated, the human heart is a "perpetual factory of idols."[11] In our fallen state we very naturally turn away from God as our source, and then we look for some promising substitute, some other "god" that will take his place. Because this god can meet our needs in only a very temporary way, our hunger actually increases, fueling an even deeper commitment to pursue that false god or find another.

Unfortunately, our commitment to these false substitutes also fills the space God himself should fill, leaving us closed and unable to receive the gifts he offers. Since he will not share his place with another, our pursuit of false gods shuts us off from the resources of the true God and only serves to amplify our hunger.

The first time I talked to Kyle about the four father gifts, I could almost see the lightbulbs turning on in his mind. His theological training and lifelong study of God's Word gave him rich spiritual resources, and he immediately understood the significance of our need for identity, love, pleasure, and place from God the Father. But when I drew out the heart diagram on a scrap piece of paper and asked him to do a quick father map of his own heart, I was surprised by his answer. His dad was a gifted Christian leader, yet in the areas of identity, pleasure, and place, he drew a picture that showed significant deficits.

"Can you tell me more?" I asked.

Kyle greatly loved and admired his dad, so it was difficult to open up about his disappointments at first. "None of our dads gave

us everything we need," I assured him. "We don't want to devalue
your earthly father but rather discover how God the Father can
more fully meet your needs."

Kyle nodded in agreement and then told me his story. His dad
put great effort into fathering but never seemed to understand how
different he was from his son. Dad was an athlete; Kyle was a student. Dad loved the world of activities; Kyle loved the world of
ideas. Dad was strong and never sick; Kyle struggled with asthma
and serious allergies.

Over and over Kyle received the message, "Just be more like me
and everything will work out great." Kyle tried with all his heart,
but he never could perform well in the areas his father valued, or
be like his dad in the ways he was strong. His dad was always there
when he had a game, giving him constant advice as Kyle struggled through various attempts at becoming an athlete and always
coming up short. Where Kyle did excel, in school and in academic
pursuits, he felt invisible, unnoticed.

I was so moved by Kyle's desire to clearly hear from his heavenly Father about his identity and place that I asked if he wanted to
spend some time in prayer together that evening. We both cleared
our schedules and went through the three steps of healing together:
awareness, cleansing, and restoration. It was a powerful time of
hearing from the Father, and the transformation in his life was so
significant that his wife wrote me several days later with news of the
tremendous change she saw in her husband.

Often after a key breakthrough we forget that growth is a lifelong process. We think one new truth will be the answer, one time
of repentance will set everything straight. Actually, we should be
glad it doesn't work that way. Growth is a gift, a treasure, an adventure. Think about other aspects of your life that are enriching.
Would you want to be finished learning new things, or building

new relationships, or collecting new experiences? Would you want to be done forever with Christmas, or never again have another birthday? Would you want to just "get over with" seeing interesting movies or learning new songs?

In the same way, getting to know the Father and receiving more of his gifts is a lifelong process that is never finished—and we should be glad about that! How could you be "finished" receiving something that is limitless, or learning something that is unfathomable?

Because of that, I wasn't surprised when Kyle called me a year later and told me the Holy Spirit had continued his counseling and shown him more he needed to cleanse. Kyle drove five hours one way to meet me, which, in itself, spoke volumes about his commitment to grow. We sat down on a bench in the corner of my yard for privacy, and I asked Kyle what the Spirit had been bringing to his mind. Kyle felt God had been talking to him about idolatry.

I knew from personal experience it takes courage to recognize when idolatry is present in your life. The fact Kyle could admit this was clear evidence of the Counselor's work. When I probed a bit deeper, Kyle told me about several defining moments in his life, as well as the present-day consequences of those situations.

Since the culture of his family was built around his dad's gifting, he had concluded as a child that this was what mattered—and that his interests and abilities didn't matter. He had come to believe he would never be able to be a person who would bring delight to his dad.

No one likes to be a disappointment, so in order to compensate, Kyle filled his thoughts with fantasies of who he would be in the future. He was determined to be great—not just great, but better than everyone else, whether as a writer, leader, or teacher. He figured he would be so great that everyone, including his dad, would have to conclude they were wrong to try and make him into somebody he wasn't—and wrong to have been disappointed in him.

When he thought about his future greatness, Kyle felt a lot better, like he at least had a "promissory note" on what he needed. Although he didn't have the praise and affirmation now, the fact that he could envision it coming was very comforting. So comforting that he started turning to this fantasy whenever he felt threatened in his identity or place.

Kyle explained how this "future Kyle" became his protector and savior. Whenever he felt vulnerable or insecure, he focused on how the "future Kyle" was going to prove them all wrong. Likewise, when he felt discouraged, he pictured how the "future Kyle" was going to be so well-known that any present failure would be part of the story of his rise to the top. When he met someone successful, he kept from being threatened by thinking about how their accomplishments paled next to those of "future Kyle."

When I complimented him for his candor, he said, "Actually, it's just embarrassing. You don't know how hard it is for me to talk about this, even though it goes on in my head all the time. I do want my life to count for God, and I do want him to give me my place. But instead I have been fighting everyone around me to make it for myself. I want my place to be significant because God created me for it, not because I am better than everyone else. Why do I have to steal place from others to make place for myself? That is just not right."

I grabbed my Bible so we could understand more about how idolatry works. We turned first to Jeremiah 17:1–2 and read: "Judah's sin is engraved with an iron tool, inscribed with a flint point, on the tablets of their hearts and on the horns of their altars. Even their children remember their altars and Asherah poles."

We talked about how idolatry burrows its way into our hearts ("engraved with an iron tool") and mixes itself with true worship ("on the horns of their altars"). It soon becomes a normal and accepted part of our lives ("even their children remember").

In Old Testament times, false gods were set up in the temple. On the way to offer sacrifices to the true God, people would stop and seek the favor of Asherah or Baal, or dash off a quick prayer to a sun god. Many times they didn't see this in conflict with their commitment to Yahweh but just as an extra bit of help where they needed it. Idolatry promises much but delivers little, since our false gods can't rescue us. The psalmist put it this way: "They have mouths, but cannot speak, eyes, but cannot see. They have ears, but cannot hear, nor is there breath in their mouths. Those who make them will be like them, and so will all who trust in them" (Psalm 135:16–18).

"Future Kyle" didn't exist, so looking to this fantasy to gain identity and place in the present was only effective for a brief time. Then reality would take over again, and Kyle would be left wondering if he would ever make it to that future destination. But idolatry doesn't just fail to deliver on its future promises; it also robs us of our current resources. Kyle was missing the joy of the journey and the appreciation of what God had given him because it constantly fell short of that superstar image that promised to meet his needs.

This is what Jeremiah described when he recorded God saying, "Through your own fault you will lose the inheritance I gave you. . . . Cursed is the one who trusts in man, who draws strength from mere flesh and whose heart turns away from the LORD. That person will be like a bush in the wastelands; they will not see prosperity when it comes" (17:4–6).

If you have ever seen pictures of the Judean wilderness, you know this is not a place where you want to spend a lot of time! These wastelands are burning hot and almost devoid of vegetation.

A bush in this rocky terrain has practically no resources to draw on. In the same way, Kyle's false god prevented him from receiving what he needed from his heavenly Father, from hearing words of *identity* and *pleasure* from him, and receiving from him the gift of *place*. Those chambers in his heart were already full, so there was no space for the Father. If God's message did not fit Kyle's image of his future greatness or ensure he would be the very best, it could not be received.

In a strange paradox, idolatry often puts us in the position of asking God to energize our false gods and then becoming disappointed when he "fails" us. Kyle would often ask God for help so he could perform at a level no one would be able to criticize; or he would ask for assistance in making "future Kyle" a reality so he could be truly secure.

But God never promised to make Kyle better than everyone else, never assured him no one would be disappointed in him. What he did promise was to be his protector and guide, his defender and deliverer. The prophet Jeremiah described in detail what the true God offers: "But blessed is the one who trusts in the LORD, whose confidence is in him. They will be like a tree planted by the water that sends out its roots by the stream. It does not fear when heat comes; its leaves are always green. It has no worries in a year of drought and never fails to bear fruit" (Jeremiah 17:7–8).

Wow, that is quite a promise from the one true God! When we trust in him we have resources that never dry up—a sure promise that our lives will never fail to bear fruit. As Jeremiah reflected on this wonderful truth, it made him realize the great tragedy of turning to false gods. He cried out to God for personal healing: "LORD, you are the hope of Israel; all who forsake you will be put to shame. Those who turn away from you will be written in the dust because they have forsaken the LORD, the spring of living water. Heal me,

Lord, and I will be healed; save me and I will be saved, for you are the one I praise" (17:13–14).

It was already dark on the bench in my yard by the time we got through these key passages. Along the way Kyle had added personal examples of the truths taught in these passages. At this point many would say, "Well, it's been great to talk. I guess I'd better go get to work on this." But Kyle already knew about the good news that ushers us into the kingdom; he knew about the power of repentance and faith.

"I guess it is time to repent," Kyle said, and I nodded in agreement. The prayer that followed was simple, focused, and powerful. Kyle named his idolatry to God and renounced it in Jesus' name. He used the images of 2 Kings 23, which describes how King Josiah cleansed the land of idols. There we read that Josiah crushed them, defiled them, ground them into powder, and tore down the altars. Kyle prayed about his idolatry using similar words, and I added my agreement as his witness.

Then Kyle turned in prayer to the Father and asked him to take the place that had been filled by these false gods. In faith he entrusted his future to him, asked him to be the source of his identity, the One he sought to please, and the Father who gives him place. What was the result of that time of cleansing? I'll let Kyle tell you in his own words:

The idol of power and fame gripped my heart from the youngest of ages. I knew it. And I fought it. I followed the theme of pride and humility through my whole Bible. I memorized verses. I talked with mentors. I read good books. I fought the idol with all of the weapons I could find. But success and freedom were always short-lived. I'd encounter an identity-questioning crisis, and find myself reaching for my idol. Once again, I'd be trapped. I gripped the idol, and the idol gripped me. That battle lasted for almost 30 years.

And then, suddenly, it broke. I now experience freedom in a way I never dreamed possible. When I lead or speak, I do it for God's pleasure, and I can feel his pleasure, like a father delighting in his son. After I teach, I enjoy the feedback of people, but I always ask God his opinion of my work, and he tells me. I engage life with much more confidence and eagerness to use my gifting.

When my heart was gripped by idolatry, I was afraid to do anything that would feed the idol. Now I have freedom to freely offer my gifts to his kingdom. I'm amazed how free I feel to not spend hours and energy feeding the idol, or trying to kill the idol. Instead, I'm free to live, to serve, to celebrate, and to rest in God's love. Those around me have noticed the difference. Short of my salvation, this was the single-most significant event in my walk with Jesus.

It may sound strange to hear someone talk about idols today, in our "civilized" world. For years I thought idolatry was just a problem in the Old Testament, or in faraway places like the Amazon jungle and the cities of India. I don't engage in any pagan rituals or offer sacrifices to some strange images like they do. Come on, I'm a Christian!

So if you are feeling a bit uncomfortable right now, I get it. I know that feeling very well. If the Counselor is already starting to put his finger on something, don't ignore it. You may need to stop right now and respond, or at least spend a little time in reflection and prayer, so you don't miss what he is stirring up in your heart. Jot down some notes so you can come back to it later and remember the details.

At the same time, if we were talking together, I would want you to know something about all five of the heart diseases before we started digging in to your defining moments. This is because all five diseases are closely interrelated, and one of them often initiates or energizes another of them. The lies about Kyle's identity sparked his idolatry, which, in turn, reinforced the lies. You'll see that is true with the next three diseases as well. I know we are dealing with demanding stuff right now—thanks for digging deep! We have covered two of the heart diseases: *lies* and *idolatry*. Now we are ready to go on to the third, the disease of *vows*.

11

TRAPPED IN VOWS

Have you ever felt so lost when trying to help someone that you had no idea what to do next? That is exactly what I experienced as I sat with Jenny and Martina, trying to make sense of the silence.

Martina had recently trusted Christ at an evangelistic camp led by Josiah Venture, our mission organization, and was being discipled by Jenny, one of our team members. Having grown up in a non-Christian family, Martina was very new to this teaching about a personal relationship with God, but she was growing like a weed. In her hunger for God, you could see all the signs of true conversion, and she was so appreciative of Jenny's investment in her life.

Then it started to happen. At strange times, usually at the end of a Bible study or right after a time of prayer, Martina would suddenly freeze. Her eyes would stare into space, her body lock in position, and she would become totally unresponsive to any external input. There was no response when asked a question, no indication she heard what people were saying, no nonverbal signs she was listening. Just a blank stare and a frozen face. It was almost as if someone had suddenly hypnotized Martina and turned her into a statue.

This would last much longer than anyone was comfortable with, and then suddenly break. She would give her head a little shake, come back to the real world, and reengage as if nothing had happened. Jenny wondered at first if she had some strange physical ailment, but Martina assured her she had never experienced anything like this before she became a Christian. Before and after the "freeze" she behaved quite normally, and there was no history of physical or mental illness that would explain her response.

Concerned about Martina and wanting to help her, Jenny asked if I could meet with the two of them and see if we could discern what was going on. Hearing her story, I suspected there might be some kind of demonic oppression taking place. Knowing how horrible it is to be under Satan's control, I began to prepare myself to confront the enemy and do battle on Martina's behalf.

When the three of us sat down to talk, I was immediately drawn to Martina's sweet spirit. She spoke openly of her faith in Christ and responded warmly to me and to Jenny. I asked about her family and probed to see if they or she had been involved in the occult. Nothing in particular came to the surface. None in her family were believers, but it also didn't seem any of them were actively engaged in occult-related activities.

I asked Martina if we could stop before going any further and ask for the Lord's leading and guidance. She nodded her head and we bowed to pray. I prayed, then Jenny prayed, and then . . . silence. We waited an uncomfortably long time for Martina to join us, then looked up to find her staring off into space—frozen.

"Martina, can you hear us?" I asked. No response. "What are you feeling right now?" I probed gently. No answer. "Is there something that is bothering you?" She was quiet. "Do you feel anything trying to take control of you?" Nothing but silence.

I looked over at Jenny, and she shrugged her shoulders. "Now you see it for yourself," she said, bewildered. "I didn't think it would happen this soon." I got up and walked to Martina's other side and called her name. She didn't turn her head. I looked directly into her eyes and tried to catch a glimmer of recognition. No response.

"Jenny, we need to test the spirits and see if there is some messenger of Satan that is stealing her voice," I said. Jenny nodded, obviously a bit nervous.

Scripture clearly tells us we are to resist the devil and he will flee from us (James 4:7). It promises that the One in us is greater than he who is in the world (1 John 4:4). We see examples in the Bible of how the disciples confronted evil spirits in the name of Jesus and commanded them to leave (Luke 9:1). We are to test the spirits (1 John 4:1–3) by seeing if they can acknowledge the lordship and deity of Christ.

These were the passages Jenny and I put into action. We prayed prayers of confrontation, resisted the enemy, took authority in Jesus' name, and asked Martina if she could submit to the lordship and deity of Christ. No change. She continued to stare out into space as if she were the only one in the room.

This did not match my previous experiences of confronting the enemy. Satan and his evil forces are described as a thief, or as a lion. Like an intruder you come upon in your house, when confronted he usually either flees or fights back. The situation either gets better or becomes much worse (see Mark 9:17–29). With Martina, it stayed the same. No response. She continued her mute stare. I looked at Jenny; she looked at me. Martina had been "frozen" for almost half an hour, and neither of us knew what to do next.

I was totally lost.

"Wow, we need some extra assistance from the Counselor right now," I said to Jenny. "Let's pray and see if he brings anything to our minds that can help us know what to do next." She nodded. It was clear she was as confused as I was. We prayed; then we listened. After a few minutes I looked up and could see Jenny was finished as well. "Did the Holy Spirit bring anything helpful to your mind?" I asked, hoping she had more than I did.

"Well," she said, hesitating. "The entire time I was praying I kept seeing a picture of a swing. I'm a visual person and often think in pictures, but I have no idea what that means, and I'm probably making it up. I'm sorry . . . that's all." She looked despondent. "What about you?" she asked hopefully.

"Not much better," I replied. "The entire time I was praying, I kept seeing a picture of a horse. That doesn't make sense, and it really doesn't help us know what to do next." I was discouraged, and I was sure Jenny could hear it in my voice. We sat there quietly, both feeling very lost. Then a voice interrupted our thoughts, a voice we had not heard in quite a while.

"I know what they mean." It was Martina. Glancing up I could see she was no longer frozen. In fact, she was looking at us and talking as if nothing had happened. "I know what they mean," she said again, forming each word deliberately and carefully.

"What are you talking about?" I asked, totally disoriented by her sudden arrival back in the room.

"The two pictures. I know what they mean."

"Well, go on," I said, leaning forward, and hoping I wouldn't do anything that would make her freeze again. Martina began to talk, the words spilling over one another as if a stream had suddenly been released. Both the swing and the horse related to early and precious memories of her father, whom she loved very deeply. This same father came home one day when she was ten and said he was leaving their family forever. I'll let you hear the story in Martina's own words, written to us in an e-mail the next day:

> I woke up this morning and had tears running down my face because of all the memories concerning swings and horses . . . These memories didn't exist until yesterday because I didn't want them to exist. They are about my father who left and . . .

Yes, I do miss him. The day he left was the very last day I cried. I came home because I wanted to give my friend a cake. My parents told me to come to the living room and asked me: Who do you want to live with? Mom or Dad? I didn't know what to say.

They told me I could choose one of them. I started to cry, I looked at Dad and said: "Mom." I wanted to run away, cry and be alone . . . but my friend was still waiting for the cake in front of our door. I wiped my eyes, took the box with the cake and opened the door. Since my dad was not going to be part of my life, I decided to pretend he didn't exist at all. I cast away all memories of him. They are back now and I am just crying and crying . . . and crying . . . because I have been holding up these tears for twelve years or even longer. I would never think the frozen moments are all about my father.

Martina was recalling one of the most important defining moments of her life. As she spoke, I tried to imagine the depth of emotion she felt on that day, the horrible realization that her world was suddenly falling apart, without warning. Her dad was leaving, and somehow in the pressure of that unexpected conversation she had also decided to leave him.

How could she process all of this? And there was her friend, at the door, waiting for the cake. In that brief moment she made a deep decision, a vow. "I decided to pretend he didn't exist at all," she said. "I cast away all memories of him." Then, before she opened the door, she made another decision so that life could go on: "I will not feel; I will not cry." It worked. "I wiped my eyes, took the box with the cake and opened the door," she wrote.

And from that day forward, for the next twelve years, she never cried.

Vows made in times of desperation have a profound impact on our lives. From our inner vantage point they bring order and sense back to a world that has spun out of control. When Martina decided to pretend her dad didn't exist, and chose to never feel or cry, her life came back into control. She could cope, continue to live, open the door, and take the cake to her friend as if nothing had happened.

But this ability to cope came at great cost. As the price to keep her vow, Martina lost a big part of herself. She was numb to her father needs, walled off from her emotion, and unaware of her loss. Vows have great power, and we will go to great lengths to keep them. Those quick vows made by ten-year-old Martina were the hidden cause behind her current "frozen" state. When someone would pray for her, she sensed the Father's touch and her emotions were stirred. Tears would well up, and she felt unexplainable long-ing for something she was missing.

But the vow bound her to keep those tears locked up, to feel no such emotion. In order to keep that vow, her unconscious self did the only thing it knew to do: freeze all responses until the danger of losing control had passed. As Martina continued to tell her story, Jenny began to weep. "Why are you crying?" Martina asked.

Jenny grabbed her hand and touched it to the tears flowing down her cheeks. "Martina, these are not my tears; these are your tears— the ones you were never able to cry." Now I was crying, and I could sense Martina was barely holding on to her promise not to feel.

"Martina, when you made that vow you knew of no other options," I said, "and you didn't know God as Father because you hadn't yet put your faith in Jesus. But now you believe in Jesus, and your heavenly Father is waiting for you to crawl up into his lap and feel his embrace. Will you cancel that vow and run into his arms?" I asked.

"How do I do that?" Martina asked.

What a great question! How do you cleanse a destructive vow? The key that opens the kingdom is always the same—repentance and faith. When you discover one of these deep decisions, repentance expresses itself first by recognizing it was a godless vow (one that was God-less, that didn't include God). Making a new decision, you cancel that vow. Then in faith you make a new one, one that includes God.

Martina nodded her head in understanding. We asked the Lord to lead her as she prayed, and then we listened as she voiced to God a beautiful prayer of repentance. I could feel shaking in the spiritual world as those chains of bondage fell off—and felt my heart leap in praise to God for his redeeming power.

After she had canceled her godless vows, we asked the Holy Spirit to give Martina the words to her new vows. They included the promise to choose the Father, to entrust her feelings to him, and to turn to him with her needs. She vowed to give him the pain of her lost earthly dad and to trust him with her tears. Jenny and I rejoiced as we heard her make new commitments, God-filled ones that were made in faith. Then we walked through the first steps of restoration, a process I will talk about in depth in later chapters. Here are more words from Martina's e-mail the next day:

> The horse leads to my father, and Jenny's "swing" leads to my father again. The only two swings I remember from childhood were at my father's grandma's. When I was in the States the people I was staying with built a great playground for the kids at the back of our house. I was home alone. I took my MP3 player and started to swing in one of the colorful swings built by such a great daddy. I was lying in the yellow tire, swinging and watching the sky . . . Suddenly I wanted God to be there

with me so much. I froze but the swing was still going up and down and I got sick. I ran inside. I came to the living room and . . . broke down.

God answered yesterday, showing me where he was every time I was crying. He did so many things yesterday. The meeting was so powerful. I have been crying all morning long. I am tired and I need to go back to bed, but I wanted to thank each of you for yesterday, for your prayers, for Jenny's tears that were actually mine ☺, for being there with me and for going through all of it with me. As Dave said—God turned my emotions on when I started to seek him. Yesterday I committed my emotions to him. So . . . O.K., I am ready to cry. Jesus is still holding me and it feels so good to cry in his arms. Finally cry . . .

Martina was no longer frozen.

After reading this story, you may be wondering, "How exactly do vows work?" or "How do I know if some vows are affecting my relationship with the Father?" In Isaiah 31 the prophet gives us key insights for understanding the nature of vows. At this time Israel was under grave threat from the mighty Assyrian Empire. Under the leadership of Sennacherib, powerful armies had already taken most of the walled cities of Judah and preparations were underway to begin the siege of Jerusalem. Messages were sent ahead to King Hezekiah to surrender or face certain destruction.

After seeking guidance from the Lord, the prophet Isaiah urged Hezekiah and his people to stay calm and quiet within the city and to await God's deliverance. The advancing army would be "terror-stricken at the voice of the LORD, when he strikes with his rod," he assured them. Furthermore, the Assyrians "shall fall by a sword, not of man" (Isaiah 30:31; 31:8, ESV).

As the huge army marched ever closer, this urging to simply trust God seemed to many as ridiculous advice. The head of the king's household, a man by the name of Shebna, convinced the nobles to prepare a "real plan" and turn to Egypt for help. They sent envoys across the desert to negotiate a promise for military assistance and shipped off large sums of money to secure this future help. Isaiah was appalled. Speaking on God's behalf, he said: "'Woe to the obstinate children,' declares the LORD, 'to those who carry out plans that are not mine, forming an alliance, but not by my Spirit, heaping sin upon sin; who go down to Egypt without consulting me; who look for help to Pharaoh's protection, to Egypt's shade for refuge'" (Isaiah 30:1–2).

Rather than rely on God, Israel made a covenant with Egypt, looking there for protection instead of to their own powerful and sovereign Lord. Vows function in a very similar way. They are strong decisions made in order to protect us when we sense a danger we feel could destroy us. Instead of turning to God, we turn to an inner promise, a "covenant" we think will deliver us.

The vows "I will cast away all memories of my dad" and "I will never cry" were covenants that gave Martina a sense of safety. When she made these powerful decisions her spinning world came back under control and she could manage life again. Like the nobles after their treaty, Martina felt protected because of her vow.

But Isaiah knew that this safety was, in fact, an illusion. The covenant would not make any difference when the enemy actually showed up at their walls. He wrote: "But Pharaoh's protection will be to your shame, Egypt's shade will bring you disgrace. Though they have officials in Zoan and their envoys have arrived in Hanes, everyone will be put to shame because of a people useless to them, who bring neither help nor advantage, but only shame and disgrace" (Isaiah 30:3–5).

What seemed to provide safety would actually bring shame and disgrace. When Martina pretended her dad didn't exist, it didn't really change anything; it just cut her off from her needs. When she "froze" to keep from feeling, people did not applaud her for being strong but wondered what was wrong with her. The vow not only is a poor protector but also costs a great deal to maintain.

To keep a vow we have to give it energy and resources, much like the people of Israel did when they sent great caravans of riches to Egypt. Isaiah wrote: "Through a land of hardship and distress, of lions and lionesses, of adders and darting snakes, the envoys carry their riches on donkeys' backs, their treasures on the humps of camels, to that unprofitable nation, to Egypt, whose help is utterly useless" (Isaiah 30:6–7).

The good news is that it is never too late to cancel a vow and make a new one. When you do, the results can be profound and far-reaching. That is why Isaiah challenged the people of Israel with these words: "In repentance and rest is your salvation, in quietness and trust is your strength" (30:15).

He knew breaking their godless covenant wouldn't be easy to do. Our vows feel like they work, and because of that it seems risky and dangerous to cancel them.

Often God has to send specially designed trials our way to help us admit our self-designed protection is not effective. A few verses later Isaiah again encourages them to turn to the Lord for help: "How gracious he will be when you cry for help! As soon as he hears, he will answer you. Although the Lord gives you the bread of adversity and the water of affliction, your teachers will be hidden no more; with your own eyes you will see them" (30:19–20).

You may be thinking to yourself at this point, "Do I have any vows that are impacting my relationship with God as Father?" Most likely you do. If the Counselor could show them to you, and you could cleanse them with repentance and faith, the result would be great blessing and freedom. In a bit I am going to show you how you can discover godless vows in your life and deal with them. But before we do, there are two more key issues we need to unpack. So far we have explored the heart diseases of *lies*, *idolatry*, and *vows*. Now let's turn to the malady of *unforgiveness*.

12

BOUND BY UNFORGIVENESS

Let me introduce you to a dear coworker in our ministry. I'll call her "Julie." She's a fruitful disciple-maker and faithful follower of Jesus. Looking from the outside, I had no idea she was carrying a heart disease that weighed on her every day. Her relationship with her father was hopelessly broken, and the pain of his rejection dripped steady poison into her soul.

From all outward appearances, Julie grew up in a model family. Her dad was successful in his work and visible every Sunday at church with his wife and four kids. Well respected in the community, he was often sought out for advice, and he even managed to teach a regular Sunday school class. But behind closed doors, the family looked very different. For as long as Julie could remember, there was serious tension between her dad and mom. The problems escalated during her fourth-grade year when Dad's problem with drinking began to really ramp up.

He started to frequent a local bar called The Office, which was creatively named to give patrons an easy way of masking their drinking habits. When asked where he had spent the afternoon, a regular could truthfully say he had been at "the office." Heading out in the evening, a man could tell his wife he was dropping by "the office" to pick up a few things he needed.

Julie's dad stopped there every day. But the trouble really began when he came home. Alcohol made him violent and aggressive, and his outbursts were so frightening that Julie often literally shook with fear. Many times she would hide under her bed, hoping he wouldn't find her there. She became terrified of the one man who should have been her protector.

Mom tried to stand up to him, but this resulted in constant arguments. Time at home was marked by permanent tension and regular outbursts of anger, coupled with yelling and door slamming. As the only girl in her family, Julie became her mom's confidante and protector, the one her mom turned to for comfort. Her mother told her all the details of her disappointment and grief, and Julie felt she had to bear not just her own difficulty but her mom's as well.

Sometimes to get away from her husband, Julie's mom would come in Julie's room and sleep with her. They locked the door for protection, but several times the ensuing outburst was so violent that both were afraid Dad would break down the door and injure them in his anger. They held each other in bed and shook with fear.

Soon others in the town were noticing his erratic behavior. Friends called and said they had seen him staggering down the street. Sometimes he would take the kids out on an errand, stop at "the office," and leave them in the car for an hour or more as he took care of some "business." Then Julie's dad received an offer for a significant promotion in his job, one that involved public representation of his company. Recognizing that his dependence on alcohol could cost him his career, he began to work at bringing his drinking under control.

Julie was in high school by this time and hoped her relationship with her dad would change for the better. But now, instead of giving all his attention to drink, he seemed to shift his addiction to work. She very rarely saw him, and when he was at home, his mind seemed to be somewhere far away. Sitting in the living room, he buried himself behind the paper or watched the news, too tired to engage with his children. Julie was very involved in school and community activities, but Dad always seemed to miss the most significant events in her life.

The tension at home continued, as well as regular fights between her parents. One Christmas the kids spent most of the evening crying, huddled around the tree while Mom and Dad fought in an adjacent room. Finally Dad moved to a basement room to get more space from his wife. There was a permanent Cold War at home.

They stayed together for the sake of appearances. In fact, few people knew the depth of the difficulty her family was experiencing. Julie felt responsible to pretend as well, to keep the secret and not betray the dysfunction in her family so they could preserve at least some facade of normalcy.

She wanted to be close to her dad, but as her mom's confidante, she seemed to always end up on the other side of the battle lines between them. One Father's Day she reached out to her dad with a special Father's Day gift, only to have it thrown across the kitchen as her dad yelled, "You're a "b**** just like your mother!"

Those words pierced like a knife.

Julie left for college. The other children grew up as well. Without the glue of the kids holding them together, her parents' relationship began to fragment even more. Dad moved out, found another woman, and then divorced her mom. Julie felt she was being rejected as well. When they met again, her dad asked her to embrace this new woman and her daughter. When Julie said that she couldn't, her dad informed her there was no place for a relationship with her.

They broke off all contact.

At this point Julie was married and had just given birth to her second child. Her dad didn't know when his granddaughter was born, wasn't even aware of her name. Julie began to see regular reunion pictures of her siblings with her dad—family pictures she was left out of. The pain of rejection cut to the core of her being. Although her dad was miles away, and Julie had a husband and family of her own, she thought about her dad all the time. Often she would cry herself to sleep at night, sick with grief, while her husband tried in vain to say something that would comfort her.

Several times she wrote long letters detailing how and why she felt so hurt by her dad, but in the end she never sent them. All she could picture coming back from him was more grief and disappointment. "I wanted him to understand and make it right," she told me later. "I felt I was right and wanted him to agree. It seemed unjust that I was suffering so much and he was moving on with life."

When Julie was pregnant with her third child, the emotions of loss became even more intense. One week she was at Bible study when the topic turned to forgiveness. Inwardly she began to fight, feeling no one else in the room really understood the kind of betrayal she had experienced. Her dad didn't deserve forgiveness. He wasn't even asking for forgiveness. How could she forgive when absolutely nothing had changed?

Then the Counselor began to speak to her. "Julie, you are the one who is suffering most from your lack of forgiveness. You are the one who needs your forgiveness, not him." Julie felt the defensiveness and resistance rising up inside her. "This is simply not possible," she told me later.

You may have felt this same resistance when the Spirit prompted you to forgive someone who has wounded or betrayed you. It's not hard to forgive someone when the offense is slight, like when a friend forgets to follow through with a commitment, or a visitor accidentally drops something on your floor. Most of us forgive like this several times during the course of a normal week. But when the offense is large, or often repeated, it becomes more difficult. When it seems the person knows what they are doing, or should know, forgiveness is much more demanding.

By forgiving, we feel we would somehow condone their actions or let them off the hook. We are concerned we will lose our right to demand a change or our ability to recover what we have lost. Most of us agree that forgiveness is appropriate; we just have a problem when an offense seems too serious or the loss too profound. This was precisely the question Peter had in mind when he asked Jesus, "Lord, how many times shall I forgive my brother or sister who sins against me? Up to seven times?" (Matthew 18:21).

I'm sure Peter felt generous about the fact that he would extend forgiveness this far. He was ready to forgive, but wanted to know the proper limits to forgiveness. "Jesus answered, 'I tell you, not seven times, but seventy-seven times' " (Matthew 18:22). I don't believe Jesus meant for Peter to pull out his calculator and start counting. His answer was intended to blow the doors off what Peter thought was generous and show him there should be no limits to forgiveness. We know this because Jesus went on to model exactly that kind of forgiveness toward us.

Then Jesus continued with a story to illustrate his point, the story of the unmerciful servant. It seems a wealthy king decided to settle accounts with his servants. Finding a rather large debt still outstanding, he called in the servant who owed him and asked for immediate and full repayment. The sum of the debt, 10,000 talents, was astronomical, equal to 200,000 years of a normal man's wages!

As you can imagine, the servant was unable to repay. Hearing that he, his wife and children, and all he owned would be sold and the proceeds put toward the debt, he fell on his knees and begged for patience and more time to gather resources. The king took pity on him and gave him more than patience. In an act of undeserved grace, he canceled the debt and let the man go free.

What an amazing gift! You would think this man would spend the next couple of years doing nothing else but rejoicing! Instead he went out and found another servant who owed him a hundred denarii—roughly 100 days' wages. Here is what happened next, in Jesus' own words: "He grabbed him and began to choke him. 'Pay back what you owe me!' he demanded. His fellow servant fell to his knees and begged him, 'Be patient with me, and I will pay it back.' But he refused. Instead, he went off and had the man thrown into prison until he could pay the debt" (Matthew 18:28–30).

Okay, this doesn't sound very good. Looking in from the outside, we are appalled at the servant's response, but these verses expose three very common symptoms of unforgiveness. Consider the servant's aggressive action: "He grabbed him and began to choke him." The first sign of unforgiveness is *inappropriate emotion.* A normal greeting on the road would be a handshake, not a throat lock! And choking does not seem to be the most appropriate way of communicating a request. Yet these kinds of strong emotions are never far below the surface when we encounter someone we haven't forgiven.

We feel angry, aggressive, strongly self-protective, and justified in causing them harm. It is easy to explode in frustration, raise our voices, or even threaten them. Our offender may be far away, but thinking of them will cause us to be flush with powerful emotion.

Julie would cry herself to sleep night after night, in spite of the fact she had a loving husband and a wonderful family of her own. Her emotional response was not rooted in the present but in past unresolved hurts of the rejection she felt from her dad.

Now, consider the servant's demand: "Pay back what you owe me!" The second symptom of unforgiveness is the *demand for repayment.* Convinced the loss was unjust, and we must somehow reclaim what was lost, we do everything in our power to get back what was taken from us. "I wanted him to understand and make it right," Julie said of her dad. "I felt I was right and wanted him to agree. It seemed unjust that I was suffering so much and he was moving on with life."

Julie would often picture in her mind what her dad ought to do to make it right, not realizing it was impossible for him to truly repay the debt he owed. Nothing would replace the protection she lost as a young girl or the affirmation she missed as a high school student. No one could undo the betrayal of his empty promises or the loss of being shut out of his life. Because of that, all attempts to get back what was lost were doomed to failure.

In the same way, the servant in this story could not repay his fellow servant, even though he fell to his knees and begged for the chance to earn back what was owed. Jesus said of the servant, "But he refused. Instead, he went off and had the man thrown into prison until he could pay the debt." Here we see the third symptom of unforgiveness: *jail tending.* Prisons are designed for two purposes—to *punish* and to *protect.* When someone is thrown into jail, we hope the punishment will convince them of the severity of their crime and teach them not to repeat it. A good prison also keeps the offender a proper distance from their victim, preventing them from continuing to injure others and making the world a safer place.

However, jail tending requires constant vigilance and energy on our part. Julie was constantly tethered to her dad and his failure toward her, even though he was physically far away. She thought about him all the time, and his presence followed her into every relationship.

When you put others in prison, the jail you design to punish them and keep yourself safe in reality ties you to that other person and makes you a slave to their choices. By placing them in prison, you actually take away your own freedom, because someone must tend their jail. Unfortunately, that someone is you. Not only that, but you also lose the benefits of the forgiveness you yourself have received.

As Jesus continued his story, he described the response of the king when he discovered the behavior of his servant: "Then the master called the servant in. 'You wicked servant,' he said, 'I canceled all that debt of yours because you begged me to. Shouldn't you have had mercy on your fellow servant just as I had on you?' In anger his master handed him over to the jailers to be tortured, until he should pay back all he owed" (Matthew 18:32–34).

This is serious! I wouldn't want to be in this servant's shoes, even more so when I read the rest of what Jesus said in verse 35: "This is how my heavenly Father will treat each of you unless you forgive your brother or sister from your heart." Notice the words Jesus used to describe God as he leaves the parable and heads back into real life for the application. He could have extended the royal metaphor by calling God the "eternal King" or the "sovereign Lord." He could have emphasized God's ownership of the universe by calling him "God, the Creator," or focused on his power by addressing him as the "Lord of hosts." Since his audience was Jewish, Jesus might have referred to God as "Yahweh," the "I AM," or as the "God of Abraham" to stress his claim on his chosen people.

Instead he calls him the "heavenly Father," a phrase never found once in the entire Old Testament. Why is this? Because unforgiveness specifically impacts your relationship with God as Father. Unforgiveness puts you in prison and makes you unable to experience the forgiveness your Father has extended to you. On top of that, it makes your Father angry because you are treating others in a way so contrary to the grace you have received from him. Dealing with unforgiveness is absolutely essential if you want to experience the fullness of a relationship with God as Father.

This is why the Counselor wouldn't let Julie rest as she drove home after her Bible study. "You need to release your dad from the responsibility to make things right with you," he told her, gently and persistently. Julie knew this was right, but she told me she didn't know what to do. "I want to forgive him, but I don't know how." She prayed, crying out for help. "Show me how."

Immediately the Counselor replied, "It is almost Thanksgiving. Julie, I want you to write your dad a letter and tell him what you are thankful for. Tell him what you appreciate about him as your dad."

This sounded like an impossible assignment, and Julie began to argue with the Lord. "God, I honestly can't think of anything," she prayed. "If you are going to ask me to do this, you are going to have to remind me, because I honestly can't remember anything good."

In spite of her inner turmoil, Julie committed herself to listen and obey. And in the next several days, God began to remind her of things she had completely forgotten: dancing to *The Lone Ranger* theme song with Dad in the living room; the time he flew to Los Angeles to meet her and take her out to dinner; the attempts he made to reach out and ask how she was doing. Then the memories began to tumble out, more than she ever could have thought of on her own.

Looking at her dad through Spirit-empowered eyes, she began to realize her father didn't know how to give her what she really needed. When she was around, he had to face the failure of his relationship with her mom, and there seemed to be nothing he could do to make it right. It was easier to disengage. Seeing him through God's eyes gave her an emotion she had never experienced toward him before.

Compassion.

At the end of the week she wrote the Thanksgiving letter; she honestly and genuinely told him what she was thankful for. With an equal measure of fear and excitement, she put it in the mail—and then waited, wondering what his response would be. Thanksgiving came. The phone rang. Julie could see from the caller ID that it was her dad calling. Her dad *never* called. She picked up the phone, trembling.

"Hi, Dad," she said tentatively. "Happy Thanksgiving."

"Hi, Julie." His voice was different, somehow more open and tender.

"I got your letter." Pause.

Julie felt herself shaking as she braced herself for his response. This was the dad she hid from under the bed, the one who exploded in anger, the one who threw her present across the kitchen. "Wow, that was really unexpected," he continued. "I don't know what else to say, but I am very thankful for this. Thank you."

Then he started to cry. Her dad didn't cry; he didn't speak tenderly; he didn't care. But there he was, on the phone, thanking her through his tears. Her cheeks were wet with tears as well—tears of relief, tears of thanksgiving.

Tears of freedom.

"I felt such a deep love for my dad, one I couldn't imagine feeling," Julie said to me later when I asked her about her breakthrough. "I was set free! I didn't hold his wrong against him anymore. I wasn't trying to get anything back from him. I released him from his responsibility to make things right, because I knew he couldn't. Forgiveness was an act of obedience," she added, "and at the beginning it was not something I felt. But when I made the choice to obey, there was lots of emotion that came after that. The blinders came off, and I was able to see Dad as Jesus saw him."

Julie went on to describe something else that happened, something she never could have anticipated: "I began to experience my heavenly Father in ways I never could before. I stopped looking to my dad for these things I needed and started looking to my heavenly Father instead. I wasn't able to receive these things from God the Father until I had released my dad of his responsibility to repay the debt. Experiencing the love of my heavenly Father blew me away. I hadn't known it before. Up until then I had never been able to taste his love or receive it. It was blocked by my unforgiveness."

Do you see the importance of forgiveness?

Unforgiveness can so easily fill the heart chambers where you have experienced father wounds or father vacuums and make it impossible for you to receive God's father gifts into this same space. By God's grace there is a way to cleanse the disease of unforgiveness. Maybe by now you've guessed what two actions open the path to freedom. Here they are again:

Repentance and faith.

Julie repented when she realized her unforgiveness was sin and not pleasing to God. She repented when she confessed her unforgiveness to the Lord in prayer and took full responsibility instead of blaming her dad or her family. This was not easy for her to do, and she had to fight through strong emotions on the path to obedience.

Then she asked the Spirit how he wanted her to live out her choice to forgive. When he gave her a specific assignment, she did it—in faith. Repentance included renouncing her right to punish her dad and canceling her claim to get back what she was owed. It included releasing him from prison and stepping down from the position of judge. She knew he was responsible to another Judge, one who is very qualified to deal with injustice and uphold what is right.

Julie's faith included ongoing choices to live in the light of forgiveness. "It wasn't a onetime thing," she said. "I had to choose to forgive Dad many times after that, because he continued to do other hurtful things. But each time, I renewed my commitment to the Lord and walked through the forgiveness process again."

Does forgiveness make a difference? You've heard Julie tell of the change in her own words. Knowing Julie personally, I have had the privilege of watching an amazing transformation take place in her life. Yes, it makes a huge difference! Forgiveness opened the way for Julie to experience a series of life-changing encounters with God as Father.

We've exposed the heart diseases of *lies, idolatry, vows,* and *unforgiveness*. Now we need to understand the poison of *sin*.

13

DECEIVED BY SIN

I met James at a conference where I was teaching on the father heart of God. A young man with lots of energy and engagement, he caught me in the afternoon break and asked to talk.

James told me he never knew his dad. Shortly after he was born, his father abandoned his wife and small child, leaving her to struggle through the challenge of raising her boy alone. Eventually he divorced her and made no attempts to build a relationship with his son.

For those who grew up having a healthy father-child relationship, it is hard to comprehend the depth of loss a boy feels when he grows up without a father. James would watch other boys playing with their dads and wonder what he had done wrong to cause his father to leave. Even a stern, demanding dad seemed better to him than a father who never appeared.

He never knew what his father looked like in person and would study the few pictures left around their house so he could memorize his face. "I wonder what he looks like now," he thought, trying to piece together some fragments of fatherhood in his mind. When he was eight, his mom told him his dad was coming to visit and take him to the store. James was giddy with delight, so full of anticipation he could hardly sleep. Finally, he would meet his dad; at last he would be able to connect with the man who was his father.

Not wanting to miss him, James decided to wait out by the gate of their house. He went out early in the morning and scanned every face that came by, in hopes it was the one. The sun was beating down, and the bugs seemed to take full advantage of his motionless state. Still, it was all worth it. He didn't want to miss out on the moment his dad arrived. But the hours passed slowly and the sun finally set. No one came.

Maybe he had been delayed. Maybe there was important work that had called him away. "Surely he will come today," James thought, as he posted himself by the gate the next morning. That day the sun and bugs were replaced by a light rain. Standing under his mom's umbrella, James spent another day by the gate. Waiting. Scanning each face that passed by as he compared it to the picture he had memorized from old photos. In the evening he trudged inside, discouraged, but not willing to give up. He waited the next day, and the next. For two whole weeks James waited by the gate.

His father never came.

Other relatives told him his father did not live too far away. In fact, someone had seen him several times in a nearby store. James couldn't understand why his only father, the one he longed to know, seemed to be purposefully avoiding him. Somehow he made it through his teenage years and graduation. His eighteenth birthday meant he could now legally represent himself. It also brought a request to show up in court. His father was not following through with the financial support he was legally bound to provide. Now he faced a formal summons to appear before the judge, and James was to be present.

In spite of the fact that these were legal proceedings, James was filled with excitement. Now he would finally be able to meet his dad! He got a fresh haircut and spent far too much time choosing the clothes he would wear to court. Sitting straight on the hard wooden bench, he reviewed the images of his dad he carried in his head, the pictures from the old photographs.

The judge entered, then the lawyers. The door opened again. In walked a man who seemed to be his dad's age. James looked at him closely. Was he the one?

Clearing his throat, the man walked over to the lawyer and addressed him. "Mr. Novak is ill today and unable to attend," he said, "so he sent me in his place. I have power of attorney to act on his behalf."

James felt his heart sink to the bottom of his feet. Not again! His dad had abandoned him so fully he wouldn't even show up to see him at the summons of a court. He slumped over in his seat, his arms wrapped around his stomach, trying to control the pounding emptiness he felt inside. "Fatherless," he said to himself. "I am totally fatherless."

When I met James at the youth conference, these events were still very fresh and painful for him. I gave time for all the young people to do a father map of their hearts and identify what they had received in the areas of identity, love, pleasure, and place. When James caught me during the break, the first thing he did was show me his map. "It didn't take too long to fill out," he said quietly. In every chamber there was a huge minus sign. "I have nothing but father vacuums," he said, dejected. "What can I do?" he asked.

I could hear the anguish in his voice. Though I was planning on preparing for my afternoon teaching, there was no doubt in my mind I needed to spend that time with James. I invited him to find a quiet place to sit, talk and explore what else the Holy Spirit had been saying to him. James said, "When you talked about the symptoms of father vacuums, I suddenly understood the reason for some of the problems I have been having."

He went on to share how he had been pulled into the downtown party scene, and how under the influence of alcohol he would often act in ways that were not honoring to Christ. Now James could see that his wild living was fueled by a search for love, by the need to belong.

He added that when I had asked the audience to write down defining moments, the Counselor had quickly brought two of them to his mind: the front gate and the courtroom. I knew we didn't have much time and wanted desperately to lead him to the Father. But I also knew we couldn't skip the step of cleansing, and it was clear there were at least two kinds of sin that needed to be cleansed: James's own sin—and the sin of his father against him.

His constant thirst for love would never be satisfied apart from a more perfect source of love—namely, the love of his Father in heaven. I explained he was trading the love of his heavenly Father for a cheap substitute, which was full of poison. In a way, he was eating the equivalent of wormy cow manure when he could be feasting at a banquet of the finest foods. I asked him why he would choose to lose so much to gain so little.

I grabbed my Bible and turned to the first chapter of John's epistle: "We proclaim to you the eternal life, which was with the *Father* and has appeared to us. We proclaim to you what we have seen and heard, so that you also may have fellowship with us. And our fellowship is with the *Father* and with his Son, Jesus Christ. We write this to make our joy complete" (1 John 1:2–4, emphasis added).

I explained that God desires for him to experience a deep fellowship with the Son, Jesus, *and* with the Father. What's more, this intimacy is a key part of the eternal life that has been promised to him and directly related to his experience of true joy. But something can block that connection to the heavenly Father. I pointed to two verses: "If we claim to have fellowship with him and yet walk in the darkness, we lie and do not live out the truth" (1 John 1:6);

"If we claim to be without sin, we deceive ourselves and the truth is not in us" (1 John 1:8).

Hiding sin and pretending it isn't wrong is a form of self-deception. After all, James wasn't fooling God—just himself. So how could he be in a position to experience his Father's amazing, mind-blowing, unlimited love if he continued to fill the emptiness in his heart with a counterfeit substitute? This made sense to James, but he didn't know how to break the sinful pattern in his life. We read on to the answer John offers in verse 9: "If we confess our sins, he is faithful and just to forgive us our sins and to purify us from all unrighteousness."

James conceded he needed to confess, but he still struggled with letting go of his false comfort because he was unsure how confession could be enough. I pointed back to the wording of 1 John 1:9 again, noting that God *promises* to forgive us and cleanse us. This isn't a promise based upon our character but upon the character of God. The Lord pledges to purify us based on his faithfulness, power, and might. How much sin will be wiped away?

The verse says, "all unrighteousness."

"I guess I'm still struggling with one thing," he said after weighing the truth of 1 John 1:9. "What if I fail again and have to confess again? I don't know if I can promise God I will be perfect."

I understood his concern. Maybe you do, too. I'd say most of us wrestle with this until we understand what John is asking us to do—as well as what he is not asking of us. John is challenging us to confess our sins and receive forgiveness and cleansing. But there is no other precondition here; there is no requirement that we never sin again. In fact, I think John may have anticipated our concern when he went on to write: "My dear children, I write this to you so that you will not sin. But if anybody does sin, we have an advocate with the *Father*—Jesus Christ, the Righteous One" (1 John 2:1, emphasis added).

In other words, the Father doesn't want us to sin. He is grieved when we turn away from his banquet of love to stuff our faces with what amounts to manure by comparison.

But perfection in the future is not a precondition for forgiveness today. In fact, as I pointed out to James, his confession showed he acknowledged Jesus was really enough, and he could turn to him again in the future if he sinned again. Not only that, but he could count on the fact that Jesus himself is fighting on his behalf to maintain an intimate relationship with the Father. He is our "advocate with the Father."

James nodded his head slowly and then asked if we could pray together. I always treasure the opportunity to join people as they exercise repentance and faith. It is a special privilege to witness breakthroughs in the spiritual world, the kind of forward steps that bring in the kingdom. James owned his sin, confessed it to God, and asked for forgiveness. In faith he committed himself to seek love from the Father rather than cheap substitutes.

"We still have some other sin to cleanse," I said when James had finished.

"What do you mean?" he answered, looking a bit confused.

"Most people don't realize this, but Jesus died on the cross not just to bear the sins you committed but also to take the poison of the sins that were committed against you." I turned to Isaiah 53, one of my favorite passages in the entire Bible, and read this aloud to James: "He was despised and rejected by men; a man of sorrows, and acquainted with grief; and as one from whom men hide their faces he was despised, and we esteemed him not. Surely he has borne our griefs and carried our sorrows; yet we esteemed him stricken, smitten by God, and afflicted" (verses 3–4, ESV).

When I asked whether there were any words in that passage he could relate to, James pointed to "despised and rejected," "esteemed

. . . not," "griefs," and "sorrows." Clearly those were words he understood through his own experiences. He found comfort in the fact that Jesus experienced rejection and grief similar to what he had suffered.

But James was blown away when I pointed to the pronoun in front of the words "griefs" and "sorrows." The passage says Jesus bore "*our* griefs" and "*our* sorrows." In other words, Jesus didn't bear a similar sorrow to James's sorrow; Jesus actually bore *his* sorrow and carried *his* grief. So great is the extent of Christ's love for us! How can we explain the fact that someone so holy and perfect would willingly take not just our sin but also our rejections, our wounds, our sorrows, and our griefs? This is incomprehensible.

Perhaps you, like James, grew up in church but never saw this before. It's easy to make the mistake of thinking Jesus' death on the cross was just about getting you and me into heaven, when in reality, he was accomplishing so much more.

The fact of the matter is that when sins are committed against us, we don't have any other hope apart from God's grace. The sins of our fathers are like poison injected into our bloodstream. It circulates through our system, affecting all parts of our being. Apart from Christ, we don't have the internal resources to cleanse the poison of sin, so it creates a constant burden, like a low-grade fever. There is only one Man who ever lived whose blood has the power to remove the sin so we can live victoriously—Jesus, because he conquered sin and death, and now his blood has the "antibodies" to cancel the effects of sin.

Look again at the words of Isaiah: "Surely he has *borne* our griefs and *carried* our sorrows . . . But he was *pierced* for our transgressions; he was *crushed* for our iniquities; *upon him* was the chastisement that brought us peace, and with *his wounds* we are healed" (53:4–5, ESV, emphasis added). In the case of my young friend James, he was bearing his own griefs and carrying his own sorrows. He was pierced by his dad's sin and was living as someone who was crushed by his father's iniquity. In a way James was bearing his own chastisement and had been trying to bring peace out of it. Clearly his wounds were still unhealed.

If you are living like James, let me say that your father's sins against you will destroy you unless and until you get them transferred onto Jesus. How do you transfer them? Through repentance and faith. On the surface this may sound confusing. You know how to confess and repent of your sins. But how do you repent for the sins that your father committed against you? They were not your sins; they were his sins, right?

It is important to recognize that our definition of repentance is often too narrow. While confession is one of the powerful expressions of repentance, it's not the only one. The Greek word for *repentance* is *metanoeo*, which literally means "after a change of mind" or "to think differently afterward."

You can't repent for your father, but you can repent for yourself. You have felt bound to carry the effects of your father's sin and have tried to process it within your own resources. That is certainly noble but ultimately also futile. If you choose to place that sin on Jesus, just as you placed on him your own sin, and let him take it to the cross and on to the grave, it will result in a transforming "change of mind." You will "think differently afterward" about all that was done against you.

This will not be a mental game but a spiritual reality. In the spiritual world you will have transferred the poison of your father's sin off yourself and onto Christ. He will swallow death in his victory and "transfuse" this victory back to you through his redeeming blood. When the offense is placed on him, the wounds are not yours; they are his. As the Bible promised, "By his wounds we are healed."

The fact of the matter is that Jesus *bore* (past tense!) our griefs and our sorrows. He has *already* taken this poison to the cross and suffered our pain on our behalf. But until we take the burden off ourselves and place it on him, the burden is still on us as well.

This, of course, is where faith comes in. Faith makes it possible for you and me to receive what has already been given to us by Christ. Our victory over sin has already been won. But by our act of faith, we draw from the resources Jesus has already prepared for us and step into the freedom he has already paid for.

At this point in my conversation with James, he suddenly understood and was ready to pray again. I challenged him to ask the Counselor to bring to mind the right words to describe the sins and offenses that his father committed against him. Some of those words are in Isaiah 53, but I knew there were more. Then, I asked James to take all of that to the cross and place it on Jesus. I said, "James, let him take the offense on your behalf. Let him bear the rejection in your place. Let him bear the iniquity and receive the full force of the sin. Then ask him to take it to the grave and defeat it. Ask him to cleanse all the effects of those sins on you with his blood. Ask him to touch your wounds and heal them. And from him, in faith, receive his cleansing and his victory."

I wish you could have heard James's prayer. It was beautiful. And even more beautiful were the changes we both immediately sensed in the spiritual world as his burden was transferred to Christ. James later described it as an almost physical experience, as if poison was being drawn out of his body and soul and then replaced with life-giving oxygen and nourishing blood.

What immediately followed were the first steps of restoration, as God the Father began to reveal himself into those two defining moments James shared at the beginning of the conversation: his deep disappointment in the courtroom and at the gate. "I feel like I am being hugged from the inside out and the outside in," James said, as he received his heavenly Father's love for the first time in his life.

"Now, how does that compare with the empty ways you have been trying to get love?" I asked. James shuddered, repulsed. Clearly there was no comparison.

The Father's love. This is what we all long for.

There is no way to go through life without getting wounded. But, like our bodies, our souls were meant to heal. When they don't, it means we have a "dirty wound," a wound that has somehow been infected by sin. If it is our sin, we have to stop making excuses, stop "deceiving ourselves," and cleanse that sin through confession and receiving Christ's forgiveness.

If those sins were committed against us, we have to realize that the cross of Christ offers resources for this poison as well. Our burden can be placed on the cross, taken with Jesus to the grave, and we can receive back from him his victory over death. This will heal us.

Understanding the resources of Christ is particularly crucial in situations of sexual abuse, a kind of sin that is profoundly destructive when committed by a father. Without a clear transfer of these wounds to Christ, it is almost impossible to piece back together the shattered remains of identity, love, pleasure, and place that were blown apart by the violation of fatherhood. Until the debris is cleared by the work of Christ on the cross, these victims are blocked in approaching God as Father. And yet, it is only in receiving the Father's identity, love, pleasure, and place that they can be healed.

Do you see the importance of cleansing? Do you see why we can't jump straight from awareness to restoration without cleansing the five heart diseases that stand in the way? Now you know all five: *lies, idolatry, vows, unforgiveness,* and *sin.* It's time to return to your story and start making this practical in your life.

14

CLEANSING THE DEBRIS

God's Word always leads you toward transformation. God's truth always draws you toward deep and lasting change. His Spirit is inviting you to take a leap of faith and walk with him though radical transformation in your relationship with God as Father.

Right now.

Your soul was meant to be filled by God's father heart and satisfied by him. Specifically, you were made to connect with God's heart as it streams toward you, filling your need for identity, love, pleasure, and place. This should not be a onetime experience but an ongoing reality, giving you roots and stability, and blessing you with abundant resources to pass on to others.

Wouldn't it be amazing if you could experience more of what your heavenly Father is offering you?

As a child, your relationship with your earthly father was designed to create certain categories and capacities, which would then be turned toward your heavenly Father and completed by him. However, our earthly fathers can get in the way of our connection with God as Father. If your dad was your hero, you might think he is enough and never turn to God to meet your father needs. Because you so admire your dad, you could also put God in a dad-shaped box, thinking your "other Dad" is the same as the one you grew up with. This is a box way too small for him.

Others have dads who create heartache, filling their hearts with debris that keeps them from connecting with God's father heart.

As you grew up, you experienced a combination of father gifts, father wounds, and father vacuums from your dad. Father gifts create *healthy giving and receiving*; father wounds cause *distortions* (the amplifier) and *self-protection* (armor). Father vacuums create *pulls* (the vacuum cleaner) and *deadness* (the corpse).

In the section on awareness, I asked you to do some father mapping—looking deeper at the state of your heart in the key areas of identity, love, pleasure, and place. Then I asked you to pick one of these areas in which you wanted to make progress. We talked about the crucial role of the Holy Spirit as Counselor, and how important it is to listen and let him reveal insights you wouldn't be aware of without his help.

Then we explored the importance of key "defining moments"—memories and experiences that were particularly formative for you. I asked you to pray and let the Counselor take you back to some of these key defining moments and review them. All of this creates awareness and prepares you for the second step of cleansing, which you are ready to begin. Now you have the opportunity to clean out the five common heart diseases of *lies, idolatry, vows, unforgiveness*, and *sin* through repentance and faith.

Whenever there is a list like these five heart diseases, I have a hard time remembering them all! If your memory is limited like mine, you can use a mental picture to help keep them straight. We know that Jesus came to give us life—meaning he wants us to live. If you remember he wants US to LIV, you can recall the five key diseases that threaten that life: **u**nforgiveness, **s**in (US), **l**ies, **i**dolatry, and **v**ows (LIV).

So how do you cleanse these five heart diseases? Your defining moments help you find and remove them. In those key memories you will find the experiences that caused you to believe *lies,* to create *idols* you thought would meet your needs, or to make *vows* you thought would protect you. Here you will find the roots of *unforgiveness* and the *sins* that you committed or were committed against you.

The bad news is that all of us are afflicted to some extent by these diseases of the heart. The good news is that they all can be cleansed through repentance and faith. How do you find out which of these diseases you need to address? Again, the role of the Counselor, the Holy Spirit, is key. Just as he brought these defining moments to your mind earlier when you prayed, so he can also bring his insight into these memories and reveal the things that need to be cleansed.

Another way to find out what hides in the darkness is to turn on the light. In the first chapter of his Gospel, John proclaims to us that Jesus *is* the light: "The true light that gives light to everyone was coming into the world" (John 1:9). When he taught the crowds, Jesus himself declared, "I am the light of the world. Whoever follows me will never walk in darkness, but will have the light of life" (John 8:12).

Have you ever tried to find something in a dark room in the middle of the night? With only a very limited sense of touch, you probably felt around in the dark like a blind person, tripping over furniture and missing things that were beyond your reach. You moved slowly and tentatively, struggling to make sense of what you were encountering. That all changed when you turned the light on. Suddenly what was hidden in the darkness became clear, and you saw the entire room and everything that was in it.

In the same way, the presence of Christ can fill each of these defining moments with light if you ask him to do this in prayer. Everything looks different when Christ is present. His truth exposes lies, his lordship unmasks idolatry, his strength shows the futility of

our vows, his forgiveness uncovers the selfishness of our unforgiveness, and his sacrifice illuminates an escape from the poison of sin.
Everything looks different in the light of Jesus.

When I work through father issues and defining moments in
my life, I usually ask a friend or my wife to join me. This is because
they bring one more set of spiritual "eyes" into the situation and
can help me see what the Spirit is illuminating. Not only that, but
I experience more clarity when I voice out loud what the Lord is
showing me. I always prefer walking through steps of repentance
and faith out loud, with someone else as a witness. It helps me when
I have to put words to my decisions and seal them with the witness
and prayers of a brother or sister.

What does this mean for you? Here is my invitation. I'll list it
out in steps so you don't miss anything:

1. Ask a friend or your spouse to set aside some time to think
    and pray with you about a deeper connection with God's
    father heart. If that is not possible, reserve a time and
    place to be alone and journal your thoughts. Make that
    journal your dialogue partner.
2. Tell them (or your journal) which of the four areas (iden-
    tity, love, pleasure and place) you want to make progress
    in, and share the symptoms you are seeing. Ask for their
    feedback and observations, or record your own.
3. Then share with them (or your journal friend) the defining
    moments God has brought to mind as you have thought
    and prayed about this. Stop and pray, asking the Spirit if
    there are any others that are important to add.
4. Pray that God the Father will transform these areas so that
    you will be able to connect with all the resources he has
    for you.

CLEANSING THE DEBRIS | 151

5. Ask the Father to show you through his Spirit which of the defining moments he wants you to start with. If you don't have a clear sense, start with the one that occurred first in your life.

6. Pray that the Holy Spirit would take you back to this moment in your mind and show you what needs to be cleansed so the Father's gifts can fill this place. Ask Jesus to bring light to this experience and to reveal his person and work into this memory. Make sure you take the time to listen after you pray.

7. Go through the list of the five common heart diseases— US LIV. Ask the Spirit to show you if any of these were formed in this defining moment or in the pattern of experiences it represents. As he reveals these to you, cleanse them with repentance and faith.

8. As I explained in the previous chapters, here is how repentance and faith are expressed with each of these diseases:

   • **Unforgiveness** – Repent of unforgiveness, calling it sin; and in faith, forgive as Christ forgave you.

   • **Sin** – If it is your sin, name it just as Jesus names it (don't deceive yourself), and ask him to forgive and cleanse you. If it is someone else's sin against you, turn from trying to bear that yourself, place it on the cross in faith, and ask Jesus to take that burden and poison from you.

   • **Lies** – Name the lie and declare in prayer that it is not true. Reject it as false and something you will not continue to believe. In faith, accept the truth. Declare in prayer that you believe the truth to be true and that you desire to live out of that truth.

- **Idolatry** – Name the idol and renounce it by calling it a false god that has no power to save you. In prayer, destroy the idol by defiling it and symbolically grinding it to dust. In faith, place the true God in the idol's place, committing your alliance to God and pledging to turn to him instead of to the idol.
- **Vows** – Renounce the vow and break it in the name of Jesus. Declare that it was a godless vow because it did not include God but represented your own effort to secure protection. In faith, make a new vow, asking the Holy Spirit for the words he wants you to use. This vow will be a vow to trust God and turn to him, relying on him alone for protection and salvation.

9. Generally, each defining moment will have several of the heart diseases, so continue to ask the Holy Spirit to reveal them until he assures you that your work there is finished. Then pray again for God's father presence to fill this place with his gifts to you. Make sure you stop and receive them, taking special note of what he is saying to you through his Spirit, through his Son, and through his Scriptures. (I will give you more about this in the next section on restoration.)

10. When that memory is finished, ask the Spirit to show you the next one he wants you to deal with. Move on to that defining moment, and go back through steps 6–10.

11. When you are finished with what the Lord wants you to deal with in this time of prayer, make sure you thank him for what he has done. Seal it by affirming again that you believe and receive what he has given to you.

12. Write down what the Lord showed you and the decisions you made. This will further solidify his work and help you

recall the details in the future. Sometimes the change is so radical and complete that it is even hard to remember how you felt before the Father cleansed that area of your heart!

Now you have clear instructions that can lead you to transformation. What will you do with them? The book of James reminds us how important it is to be "doers of the Word" and not merely "hearers." If we don't put God's Word into practice, we are like a man who looks at his face in the mirror and then walks away, forgetting what he saw (James 1:22–25, ESV). Without personal application, not only will all your investment in reading this book make no difference, but you will also soon forget what you learned.

Will you be a "doer"? Who will you invite to join you? When will it be?

Stop and make those decisions now, before you read on. Don't look in the mirror and walk away. The Father is waiting to meet with you in a much deeper way than you have ever known.

15

DARING TO DRAW NEAR

When my middle son, Caleb, celebrated his twenty-first birthday, I knew we needed to mark this milestone in a special way. So I took him to a snow-covered mountain with over 4,000 feet of vertical drop, and we carved up the slopes together. Caleb is a snowboard man; I am an old-school skier. But we both enjoy whatever is steep and deep. We took turns finding new routes through the trees and hollered with delight as we swooped through evergreens loaded with powder. On the lift riding up, I prayed that God would notice how much fun this was and decide to offer skiing in heaven.

That night my wife, Connie, and daughter, Claire, prepared a special dinner and cake for Caleb. They covered the table with balloons. After Caleb opened presents, we gave him the gift of words, sharing what we appreciate about him and highlighting the ways he had grown in this past year. I told him that he has become a man.

"You are not afraid of risks and love adventure," I said, "but at the same time, you have developed great judgment and wisdom. Courage and wisdom—those are important qualities for a man. You are ready to lead a family!" I said. He smiled broadly, and we all knew he was thinking of his bride-to-be, Haley.

"I can't wait to lead her and follow the Lord together," he said. "Just four more months till the wedding!" Then Caleb became thoughtful. "Dad, was there anything you were concerned about when I was a kid?" he asked.

"Well, yes, there was," I answered. "You were always so full of passion and emotion; we often said you wore your heart on your sleeve. But those same emotions would get the best of you, and you would be overwhelmed by them, falling apart into a puddle of helplessness."

"What did you do?" Caleb asked.

"Anything we could think of," I said, laughing. "But it was crazy—if you and I could just get focused father-son time together, you would settle down and stabilize out. It was like being together, just the two of us, re-centered you."

"It still does, Dad," Caleb said quietly. "Like today. You should write about that in your book." So here it is—I took his advice.

There is something about a true father connection that goes beyond words. It is richly nourishing and deeply meaningful—for both the parent and child. All my kids are grown now, but I'm still their dad and will be all their lives. As the leader of a mission organization, I have many pressing responsibilities, but none are more important than being the father to my kids. I think about it every day.

Shortly before Caleb's birthday, my daughter, Claire, joined us for Christmas break. She loves photography, so one afternoon I stole her away for a daddy-daughter date to a park filled with massive red rocks. Wandering through the breathtaking vistas covered with snow, we tried to capture the right angles for the perfect shot.

Then we set the camera on a tripod and did silly pictures of the two of us with cottonwood trees and red cliffs in the background. With the camera's timer set, we tried to launch into the air together at just the right moment when the shutter would open. Of course, it was almost impossible to time it right, so most of the pictures captured us futilely trying to get in position, or laughing hilariously at our missed attempts.

Since the camera was on one side of a small road and we were on the other, our photo session was often interrupted by a car passing by. "I wonder what they think we are doing," Claire commented. "But then again, I really don't care," she continued with a mischievous grin. I heartily agreed. Later she edited the pictures for her very creative blog, and we talked together about how to get a website up for her new photo business, ClairelySeen Photography. I encouraged her to go for it, since it helps her take her skills to the next level, and might provide some extra income while in college. She agreed and started right in.

My last thoughts that day were about how much I enjoy being a father.

Shortly after that, I called my oldest son, Tyler. He is married now and studying for his master's in Old Testament theology at Trinity Seminary. After struggling so hard myself to learn Greek, I'm amazed he actually enjoys mastering the intricacies of the Hebrew language. Tyler enjoys the challenge of learning something new. He has always been one to focus on a new skill until he excels in it.

"So how were your first days at Intelligentsia?" I asked. Tyler had just been hired at a prestigious coffee shop in downtown Chicago, and I guessed he was reveling in a new opportunity to master the art of a perfect cup of coffee.

"Dad, it was amazing!" Tyler said, and then he hurried on to explain his new insights into roasting techniques, proper grinding, and the fine art of tuning the extraction. I loved hearing it all and asked lots of questions. Most of all, I was filled with pride and joy for my son, and delight in how God made him.

After asking about his Christmas visit to his in-laws, and checking in on a couple of things he had asked us to pray for, I turned the phone over to my wife. "Tyler sure enjoyed talking with you," she said when they were finished. "It meant a lot to him that you called."

"It meant a lot to me too," I said. "I love talking with my son!"

I really do love being a father. My own experience helps give me insights into what my heavenly Father must think and feel toward me. Here is some of what is important to me as I care for my children:

- I treat each one of them differently, based on their personality, interests, and stage of life.
- I enjoy who they are.
- I initiate conversation and time together.
- I am always thinking about how to open the way ahead of them.
- I love to support and encourage them.
- I am not afraid to give correction and advice.
- We talk openly about their weaknesses and where they need to grow.
- They know I believe in them.
- I follow what is going on in their lives and pray for them.
- I let them in on what I am thinking and experiencing, and consider them some of my closest friends.

Why am I sharing this? According to the Bible (and confirmed by my experience), I am a flawed, limited, sinful, and inadequate dad. If a flawed, limited, sinful, inadequate dad cares this much about fathering, how much more does your perfect, unlimited, sinless, fully adequate heavenly Dad care about being a father to you? Do you realize how important this is to him and how meaningful it can be for you?

In his first letter, the apostle John tried to stop us in our tracks with these words: "See what great love the Father has lavished on us, that we should be called children of God! *And that is what we are!*" (1 John 3:1, emphasis added). Now that you have some of the junk cleared away from your work on cleansing, you can start to be overwhelmed by the riches of what the Father wants to do and be for you.

When my son Caleb was a small boy, any time I was on the floor in the living room issued an open invitation to a running, full-body hug. He would wind up across the room, lower his head, and then come barreling toward me, knocking me over with a maximum contact embrace. Then we would "wrestle" for a few minutes on the floor, grunting and groaning in what was really just an excuse to be manly and close. There was nothing held back in these crashing father-son encounters, no checking twice or being careful. After a bit, Caleb would climb off, sweating and grinning, only to circle to the other side of the room and come barreling toward me again.

Do you run toward the Father with that kind of abandon?

"Oh, but that is different," you may say. "God is almighty, powerful, a King. You don't approach someone like him that way." If it weren't for Jesus, that would be true. But because of him, the writer of Hebrews urges us to "approach God's throne of grace with *confidence, so that we may receive mercy* and find grace to help us in our time of need" (4:16, emphasis added). In Ephesians Paul tells us, "In him and through faith in him we may approach God with *freedom and confidence*" (Ephesians 3:12, emphasis added).

Freedom and confidence. That sounds to me like a "running, full-body hug." But if you are like most people, you hold back. You don't run toward the Father with abandon. You don't press in to get as close to him as possible. You don't expect joy and pleasure in his presence but wonder if he may be harsh or uncaring with you, or somehow push you away. This causes you to hold back, to wait, to turn your head away.

As we work toward restoration of the Father relationship you were meant for (the third step in our process), it is important that you understand something more about how Jesus and the Holy Spirit are both actively working to bring you close to the Father. Of course you will need to respond to their work. You will need to believe and receive something from them so you can dare to draw near.

Think about the amazing relationship Jesus had with his Father. It was the perfect father-child relationship, full of intimacy and goodness, and rich with meaning. Listen to some of the things Jesus said about his Dad:

- "Do you think I cannot call on my Father, and he will at once put at my disposal more than twelve legions of angels?" (Matthew 26:53)
- "Abba, Father," he said, "everything is possible for you." (Mark 14:36)
- "Why were you searching for me?" he asked. "Didn't you know I had to be in my Father's house?" (Luke 2:49)
- "And I confer on you a kingdom, just as my Father conferred one on me." (Luke 22:29)
- "The Father loves the Son and has placed everything in his hands." (John 3:35)
- "My Father is always at his work to this very day, and I too am working." (John 5:17)
- "The Father who sent me has himself testified concerning me." (John 5:37)

Perhaps it was watching this amazing relationship that caused Philip to say, "Lord, show us the Father and that will be enough for us" (John 14:8). Looking in on Jesus with his Father made Philip long for a bit of that same blessing. But Jesus went way beyond what Philip expected in his answer. First of all, Jesus reminded him that he was in the Father and the Father was in him. Because of that, anyone who had seen Jesus had seen the Father (John 14:9–11). They were so close that all of the Father was also in the Son. What an amazing relationship!

Then Jesus promised he wouldn't leave his followers as orphans, that he would come again to them. He told them, "Because I live, you also will live. On that day you will realize that I am in my Father, and you are in me, and I am in you" (John 14:19–20).

Whoa, did you catch that? We already heard Jesus say he was in the Father and the Father was in him. But now he uses that same language to say we are in him and he is in us. Because we are placed in him, and he in us, we are suddenly joined to this amazing relationship he has with the Father. We are in Jesus, Jesus is in the Father, and Jesus is in us.

We are as close to the Father as Jesus is.

Are you kidding? How close is that?

As close as we could possibly be!

Don't miss this. It is only through Jesus that you can draw near to the Father. That is why Jesus said, "I am the way and the truth and the life. *No one* comes to the Father *except through me*" (John 14:6, emphasis added). If you try to get into the Father's presence on your own, you'll never make it. There is no other way except through Jesus.

If you take that "way," if you believe and receive what he has done for you on the cross, you are immediately placed right in the middle of his relationship with the Father. Where you were once far away and estranged, you suddenly become just as close as Jesus. The amazing relationship with the Father that Jesus had is the same relationship that is now yours.

This truth is so important for you to understand. You do not come to the Father on your own terms; you come through Christ, clothed in him, washed by his blood, redeemed by his sacrifice, covered by his grace. This "way" takes you all the way—there is no other way to get close to him. So often we try to press into the Father's presence on our own merit, or we hold back as we sense our inability to truly commend ourselves to him. Instead we should believe and receive what Jesus offers us, and run to the Father clothed in the Son.

Sometimes we hold back in fear. But as John said, "There is no fear in love. But perfect love drives out fear, because fear has to do with punishment. The one who fears is not made perfect in love" (1 John 4:18). What frees us from the fear of punishment? Listen to this: "Therefore, there is now *no condemnation* for those who are in Christ Jesus, because *through Christ Jesus* the law of the Spirit who gives life has set you free from the law of sin and death" (Romans 8:1–2, emphasis added). It is through Christ Jesus we are freed from all condemnation and have no reason to fear! Believing and receiving the work of Christ always precedes intimacy with the Father.

"Okay, I know all about Jesus," you may be saying. "I put my trust in him a long time ago when I was saved. Shouldn't that be enough?"

Believing and receiving Jesus begins at salvation—but it doesn't end there. Paul wrote, "So then, *just as you received Christ Jesus as Lord, continue to live your lives in him*, rooted and built up in him, strengthened in the faith as you were taught, and overflowing with thankfulness" (Colossians 2:6–7, emphasis added).

The same faith in Christ that brought you salvation also continues to be the means by which you experience more of the riches of the Father. That is why you must guard against trying to get closer to the Father in any way other than through Christ. Paul warned of this in the next verse: "See to it that no one takes you captive through hollow and deceptive philosophy, which depends on human tradition and the elemental spiritual forces of this world rather than on Christ" (Colossians 2:8).

You see now that Jesus is actively working to draw you closer to the Father. But the Spirit is also at work, helping you to understand and experience what the Father offers. When you trusted Christ, his Spirit was placed inside of you. It is this indwelling presence that gives you the ability to hear and understand what God the Father is communicating to you. Look at what Paul wrote in Romans 8:14–17:

> For those who are led by the Spirit of God are the children of God. The Spirit you received does not make you slaves, so that you live in fear again; rather, the Spirit you received brought about your adoption to sonship. And by him we cry, "*Abba*, Father." The Spirit himself testifies with our spirit that we are God's children. Now if we are children, then we are heirs—heirs of God and co-heirs with Christ.

The Spirit leads you. The Spirit testifies to you about your sonship or daughtership! The Spirit empowers your spirit to cry out, "Abba, Daddy." The Spirit helps you receive your inheritance.

Not long ago I was in Israel and wandered into a Jewish bookstore. Browsing through some books written in English, I caught a typographical mistake. They had missed the letter *o* in a paragraph that included the word *God*, spelling it "G*d." I thought this was strange and couldn't believe the publisher actually allowed this book to go to print with such an obvious mistake. Reading farther down the page, I caught it again: "G*d." They kept leaving out the vowel in the word *God*. Talk about careless!

Then I suddenly remembered what I had learned in Bible college about the Jewish respect for God's name. Not wanting anyone to mistakenly take God's name in vain, the Jewish scribes left out the vowels in the Hebrew word *Yahweh* as they copied the scrolls, writing it as *Yhwh.* This was a sign to the reader to stop and not speak God's name carelessly. Evidently in these English books, they were continuing this tradition. To these Jews, God is holy, mighty, transcendent. Any mention of his name must be done with proper and due respect.

After browsing through the store, I continued my walk through the winding narrow streets of Jerusalem. An Orthodox Jewish family passed me, all dressed in black, the man wearing an old-world felt top hat with long, curly locks of hair spilling out under each side of the brim. His young son held his hand as they scurried through the street, wearing a skullcap and showing some early locks of his own. They spoke to each other earnestly in Hebrew. I couldn't understand a word.

Then I heard it.

"Abba," the young boy said as he looked up at his dad and continued with what seemed like an important question, though it was unintelligible to me. "Abba." The word came again as they trotted down the street, hand in hand.

"Abba." "Daddy." The most informal and intimate expression from a child to his or her father. In a culture where God's name cannot be written in full because it is so holy, a young boy calls his father "daddy." Because we have been adopted into God's family, the Spirit of this awesome transcendent God causes our spirit to cry out these same words.

"Daddy!"

This is almost too amazing to comprehend.

As you dare to draw near to the Father through Jesus, his Spirit will be speaking to you from within, assuring you that you belong to him, and empowering your spirit to actually *experience* that reality. You may be caught off guard by the emotions you feel, or surprised by the intensity of what you experience. It may not feel like you, because it is not you. God's Spirit is actively stirring your spirit, giving you the ability to call out "Abba" in a true and genuine way.

Sometimes we reduce our relationship with God to a set of truths we hold to or a body of information we master. We are like spectators in an audience watching a play. God is the subject of our observations, the object of our inquiry. As we watch, we try to file away what we have learned. Then we applaud, gather our things, and go home.

This is a far cry from what the Bible teaches. Instead of mere spectators, we find we are the subjects of the Father's love; instead of observers, we learn we are the objects of his grace and mercy. He himself takes center stage and then suddenly pulls us into his story, as the saints who have gone before us and the angels all look on. They are the spectators; we are swept up into the drama. They cheer and applaud; we launch into dance like a bride swept off her feet by her groom.

Remember my stories at the beginning of this chapter—the ski day with Caleb, photography with Claire, and the phone call with Tyler? Each was about much more than just information. Those father connections included experience, emotion, conversation, laughter, touch, and the gift of presence. What God your Father wants to give you includes all of these and much, much more.

It is possible because you are in Christ. Believe and receive what he has done and is doing for you. It is real because the Spirit is working inside of you. Believe and receive his ongoing words of testimony to your spirit. Then gather yourself, and run toward the Father, abandoning your fear as you lunge toward a full-body embrace.

16

THE SPIRIT OF WISDOM
AND REVELATION

Have you ever prayed a really bold, faith-filled prayer, one that courageously asked God for miraculous things only he could do? Perhaps you recall a prayer where you stepped out in faith to ask God for significant financial provision, or pleaded with him for supernatural physical healing. Maybe you prayed for open doors when your way was blocked, or for God-sized solutions to impossible problems.

Paul prayed two really bold, faith-filled prayers in the book of Ephesians, but the focus of these prayers might surprise you. They are not prayers for problems to be solved or for financial needs to be met. They are not prayers for physical healing or for open doors. Both of Paul's bold, faith-filled prayers are "father prayers."

A man of unusual insight and amazing courage, Paul could have asked God for anything as he prayed for the believers in Ephesus. No doubt he was aware of many challenges they were facing and urgent needs that were pressing them down. With all these possibilities in mind, he chose to pray two amazing prayers that centered on just one thing—how they could experience the fullness of deep connection with the Father.

I'd read through these prayers many times before I fully understood their importance. It wasn't until I started to take them at face value, and apply them personally, that I was blown away by their significance. In fact, it was only when I began praying these prayers for others and expecting God to answer them that I started to see people have life-changing encounters with the fatherhood of God.

Are you curious? I hope so. These two prayers will take a bit to fully understand and require bold faith on your part. You'll need to think about what Paul was saying and have the courage to expect God will actually answer. These two prayers may very well be more important than any other bold, faith-filled prayer you have ever prayed—other than, of course, your prayer to accept Christ.

Let's look at the first one. Read the entire prayer below, and then we will start to dig into it and discover what it means:

> For this reason, ever since I heard about your faith in the Lord Jesus and your love for all God's people, I have not stopped giving thanks for you, remembering you in my prayers. I keep asking that the God of our Lord Jesus Christ, *the glorious Father*, may give you the Spirit of wisdom and revelation, so that you may *know him better*. I pray that the eyes of your heart may be enlightened in order that you may know the hope to which he has called you, the riches of his glorious inheritance in his holy people, and his incomparably great power for us who believe. (Ephesians 1:15–19, emphasis added)

From the first lines of this prayer we know Paul is praying for people who have a living faith in Jesus Christ and loving relationships with other believers. My guess is that is also true of you. Like Paul, I am thankful for that! At the same time, Paul is not content to leave them there. He wants something more for these dear brothers and sisters. He asks God—in fact, he *keeps asking God*—for a particular gift. Paul makes it clear this is a prayer to the Father; he calls him the "glorious Father" as he makes his request. What does Paul ask for?

The Spirit of wisdom and revelation.

What does this mean?

Wisdom is different than knowledge or understanding. Knowledge comes as we gather information; understanding is gained as we comprehend it. Wisdom, however, takes knowledge and understanding one step further. Wisdom is not just truth known or truth understood. Wisdom is truth applied.

A wise man or woman has the ability to accurately assess a situation, know which truth needs to be brought to bear, and correctly apply the truth to that particular reality. Wisdom is standing at a locked door and knowing which key will quickly open the way. Wisdom is lifting the hood on a stalled engine and knowing what tool or part will get it running again. Wisdom is knowing what words will shed light on a confusing problem and illuminate a way out of a tangled mess.

So, we better start learning this wisdom, right? Yes, wisdom is something we can develop and a skill we can learn. But look closer at the kind of wisdom Paul is talking about here. He wants the believers to receive "the Spirit of wisdom." This wisdom is the kind that comes directly from the Spirit, wisdom that is brought to us from outside of us by the Spirit of God.

When it comes to father issues, you probably already know many truths you are unable to apply. You know them in your head, but you don't believe them in your heart, at least not in the places where visceral and emotional convictions are formed. You know in your head that the Father is with you, yet you feel all alone. You have heard many times that he loves you, but you still feel forgotten and unloved.

This is exactly what David was talking about when he said, "Behold, you delight in truth in the inward being, and you teach me wisdom in the secret heart" (Psalm 51:6, ESV). David knew he needed to not just know truth but know it in the right places. God wanted truth to be found in his "inward being," in the "secret heart." He called this "wisdom." So how do you get truth off the page and into the spot where you need it the most? How do you take convictions you have in your head and turn them into visceral and emotional convictions of your heart?

We'll get back to that in a moment, but first we need to understand the other part of Paul's request. He asks for "the Spirit of wisdom *and revelation.*"

What is revelation? Sometimes television series will work to keep our attention by building up tension toward a big "reveal." A group of contestants has been battling to take off weight, and we have followed their progress for several months. Then they are sent off by themselves to complete the last leg of their weight loss in secret. For many weeks they spend hours in training and make hundreds of decisions to eat right and persevere. We, however, have seen none of this and have no idea of the outcome.

A huge crowd gathers. The announcer breathlessly reminds us of what is at stake. The winner can claim a radically transformed body—and a rather large check. We lean forward in our chairs as a life-size picture of each contestant is brought onto the stage, a picture of what they looked like before the competition began. What do they look like now? None of us know.

The music builds, and suddenly one of them bursts through the picture of themselves. We all (hopefully) gasp. The "reveal" has come! In an instant, we see the outcome of all that has gone on behind the scenes. In a moment, we realize they are half the size they used to be, brimming with energy and renewed health. What was hidden from our eyes has now been revealed! It only takes a moment to comprehend, because we can see it for ourselves. We soon know without a doubt who is the biggest loser!

Other game shows capture our attention with curtains that are closed, or boxes that have not yet been opened. Contestants compete to win "curtain number one," or they have to make risky choices to choose "box number three," all without knowing what is inside. Then the obligatory lovely assistant directs our attention to the curtain that is about to open, or the box that is ready to be lifted. We all wonder what is inside.

Ta-da! The curtain opens, the box lifts, and in an instant we see what was hidden from our sight. Sometimes we groan in disappointment at the poor choice that is suddenly revealed or cheer with delight at the amazing good fortune that has now become so clear. Revelation does not create something new; it reveals what is actually there but previously hidden from our eyes. It breaks through the limited "picture" we hold as true and shows us the result of what was going on "behind the scenes," out of our sight. Revelation lets us in on God's perspective; it helps us comprehend more fully what he has been doing.

Revelation "pulls the curtain" and "lifts the box" so we can perceive the true nature of things. It makes it possible for us to see what has true value and what, in spite of its lavish appearance, is actually worthless.

"Okay," you might be saying, "but I don't understand what this practically means. Am I supposed to start having visions like Daniel or hope to get swept up to the third heaven like Paul?"

Look back to the rest of the prayer. Paul goes on to ask that "the eyes of your heart may be enlightened." He is asking the Father to enlighten, or turn on the lights for, your *spiritual eyes*, the "*eyes of your heart.*" It seems there is an inner sight that gives you the ability to see into the spiritual world in a way that illuminates your heart, the very core of your being. Did you know your heart has eyes? If these spiritual eyes are not currently perceiving anything, you may need "the Spirit of wisdom and revelation" to turn the lights on. God's purpose in this is that you would "know [the Father] better."

Remember Brian?

I told you part of his story in chapter 8. Just to refresh your memory, Brian was a successful financial manager, community leader, and elder at his church who seemed from the outside to have it all together. Then God led him into a significant family crisis. His unwed daughter came home with the news that she was pregnant, then lost the baby and spiraled into depression. Rather than engaging, Brian withdrew in fear, unable to lead his family and locked up in fathering his hurting daughter.

I told you that we asked the Counselor (the Holy Spirit) to show us where this block was coming from, and he reminded Brian of four key defining moments from his childhood that had tremendous significance. Brian had lost his dad when he was just twenty months old and never connected with the man his mom later remarried. He grew up "fatherless" and felt that vacuum every day.

Even at age fifty-four he saw himself as a man with a gaping hole inside, a man without the resources he needed to be whole. Competent on the outside, he lived in fear that others would discover he was really an impostor, a man who was hollow and missing the core of his being. Where his heart needed identity, love, pleasure, and place, Brian experienced painful silence. His earliest defining moment was a memory at two and a half years of age, when his mom left for work and he broke down in uncontrollable sobs in the living room, feeling utterly abandoned and destined to be forever alone.

I told you how the Counselor revealed the lie he believed in that place, the lie that had convinced Brian he was alone and would always be alone. We prayed God would reveal his father presence into that same place in his heart. This was the first Ephesians "father prayer," the request for "the Spirit of wisdom and revelation, so that you may know [the Father] better."

I asked Brian to look at this memory through the "eyes of his heart" and let me know when he sensed, felt, heard, or saw the presence of the Father. I also shared with him that if the Father revealed himself in physical form into that experience, it would be in the person of Jesus, since "no one has ever seen God, but the one and only Son, who is himself God and is in closest relationship with the Father, has made him known" (John 1:18).

After a moment of silence, Brian suddenly said, "Oh, he is there."

"Where?" I asked.

"In the corner of the room."

"What is he doing?" I asked him.

Then Brian began explaining, as if describing an unfolding scene in a movie, how Jesus, putting flesh on the Father, came to him and sat down beside him on the floor. Wiping his tears, he began to reassure him that everything was under control, that he was not alone. Jesus told Brian, in simple words and actions perfectly designed for a two-and-a-half-year-old, that he was not abandoned, that he was with him and would always be with him.

It was then that the Holy Spirit began to bring verses of truth to both of us and we started to look them up and read them aloud together. I shared these with you in chapter 9, but let me list a couple of them again: "Though my father and mother forsake me, the LORD will receive me" (Psalm 27:10); "Never will I leave you; never will I forsake you" (Hebrews 13:5); and, "A father to the fatherless, a defender of widows, is God in his holy dwelling. God sets the lonely in families" (Psalm 68:5–6).

Do you see what was happening? God was giving Brian *the Spirit of wisdom* (truth from the Spirit, applied perfectly to his situation) *and revelation* (the curtain was removed so he could perceive the presence of the Father). These truths and this reality had always been there, but they were hidden from his sight. The Spirit of wisdom and revelation opened the eyes of his heart.

Now Brian could reject the lie that he was all alone and receive the truth of God's unending care into his inmost place. Now this was not just information in his head but a deep and visceral conviction in his heart. Sometimes this Spirit of wisdom and revelation precedes cleansing, since we need the light of God's illumination to be able to see and respond to the diseases of the heart. Other times the cleansing must come first, because we are unable to even sense the Father's presence until the poison is removed.

It is important to not let your expectations preempt the way God wants to reveal his father heart to you. Sometimes it is through the person of Jesus, like Brian experienced. Other times it is simply a stream of emotion, such as the story I told about James when he said, "I feel like I am being hugged from the inside out and the outside in!"

Sometimes it is through a passage of Scripture that the Spirit brings to mind in a way that you know was sent from the Father as his message for you. Other times, the Spirit may bring specific words from the Father that are custom designed for your situation. All of this, of course, will be in 100 percent agreement with the Word of God, which is your final authority and standard for truth.

The Father has many ways to reveal himself and will use them all, communicating his father heart in ways that match his perfect assessment of what we most need. Brian and I were not alone as we talked and prayed through his key defining moments. His good friend and coworker, Alan, had joined us at my request, since I know that Alan had much to offer through his deep walk with God and loyal friendship.

One of the key defining moments the Spirit brought to Brian's mind was an important softball game when Brian was ten years old.

A natural athlete, Brian had made the all-star team, playing a key role at third base. But, as always, neither his mom nor his stepdad had come to watch the game. Brian began to tell us the story. "Halfway through the inning there was a pop fly to left field," he said, obviously reliving the experience in his mind. "I'm running back full speed and make a diving catch. It was like something you see in a picture out of *Sports Illustrated*. I'm stretched out full length in the air, my glove reaching for the ball, and somehow I catch it. I get up, the ball is in my mitt and—"

Brian's voice trailed off. He tried to continue but was too choked up with emotion to speak. Alan quietly finished his sentence: "And there was no one there to see it."

Brian nodded. His shoulders began to shake with silent sobs.

I closed my eyes and prayed out loud. "Father, Brian needs to meet you in this place. He needs what only you can give him. Reveal yourself to him. Show him where you are and what you are doing." It was quiet. Nothing. I continued to pray silently, feeling a mounting sense of desperation. I pleaded for the Spirit of wisdom and revelation. Then I heard a noise and looked up. I saw Alan rising from the couch and stepping directly over the wide coffee table that stood between him and Brian.

"Stand up," he said to Brian brusquely. My eyes widened with surprise. Climbing over a coffee table and barking orders at his friend seemed very out of character for a highly analytical, generally quite-reserved type of man like Alan. Brian looked up from his prayer, obviously confused. Wordlessly, he rose from his chair. When he reached full height, Alan immediately wrapped him in a bracing hug, the kind football players give each other after winning a game. Then he spoke in a strong, emotion-filled voice, "On behalf of your Father, I am so proud of you!"

We all wept.

God knows how to reveal himself to us, and he can do it in ways we don't expect. Brian was missing father pleasure, the joy and pride that come from an engaged father's heart. This time, God chose to reveal his truth through one of his servants, putting his message into skin and giving it a voice. All of us knew that the Father had spoken.

He continued to speak, revealing Christ's presence in the stands, rooting Brian on. In this moment and in several other defining moments, God spoke other father words directly to Brian through his Spirit. As Brian voiced what the Father was telling him, his friend Alan wrote the words down quickly on a yellow pad, capturing them for Brian to review later on. This is what the Father said:

I'm so proud of you.
I am watching. I know. I care.
This is not your home, I AM. I am going with you.
I am with you just as I was with your dad. This is part of
my plan. This is your heritage.
You are in your father's stream of spiritual blessing.
Listen to me, I am your Father. No counterfeits allowed.
Seek my pleasure. No one else's. Seek it. I give it to you.
It is possible to please me. Simply trust me.
Engage with people. Don't try to fix their problems.
Trust me. I will.
You are my responsibility.
Brian, I am trustworthy.

Did these words from the Father make any difference? Six months after his breakthrough, I was talking on the phone with Brian's boss, the founder and president of a private equity fund. "I don't know what you, Brian, and Alan did together," he said, "but the change in Brian has affected every area of his life. He has become confident, engaged, centered. In fact, I would say that his value to me on this team has increased tenfold."

That was four years ago. Recently I met with Brian over coffee to ask him about the long-term impact of learning to connect with God's father heart. Here is what he said:

Then – I was self-protecting, fear based, alone. I was often in a deep funk. I would withdraw, going on the weekends to what I called my "happy place," which wasn't too happy. Just total withdrawal, trying to process what happened during the week, but it was not good.

I felt like I was engaging alone, focused on image management, positioning. In everything I was concerned about how things reflected on me. God was faceless. I could not see a face on God. I didn't want you to figure me out. I felt like I needed to compete and get my way.

Now – I'm experiencing the flow of the Father's love and care; whatever the opportunities are, it is up to him. I'm walking into situations with more courage; I'm more vulnerable. I have nothing to hide—I don't feel that I have ANYTHING to hide at all, for which I am very thankful. I feel there is greater awareness of opportunities to engage with people. I'm less "ends" focused and more focused on impact. What others think has far less impact on me.

There is a sense of being with him, identity in him. I feel much more relaxed. I am working out of strengths and have a better sense of submission. Not alone. Not responsible for fixing what's broken, more in the mode of just loving as a husband and dad.

Then Brian summed it all up with just one phrase: *"I feel like God has given me back my inheritance."*

Do you remember the rest of the father prayer? "I pray that the eyes of your heart may be enlightened in order that you may know the hope to which he has called you, the *riches of his glorious inheritance* in his holy people, and his incomparably great power for us who believe" (Ephesians 1:18–19, emphasis added).

God had answered our bold, faith-filled prayer.

This does not mean Brian has arrived or stopped growing. The second father prayer in Ephesians tells us that we can always go deeper in our understanding and experience of God's love. Look carefully at this prayer, found in Ephesians 3:14–19 (emphasis added):

> For this reason I kneel *before the Father*, from whom every family in heaven and on earth derives its name. I pray that out of his glorious riches he may strengthen you with power through his Spirit in your inner being, so that Christ may dwell in your hearts through faith. And I pray that you, being rooted and established in love, may have power, together with all the Lord's holy people, to grasp how wide and long and high and deep is the love of Christ, and to know this love that surpasses knowledge—that you may be filled to the measure of all the fullness of God.

God will have to strengthen you with power in your inner being so you can even begin to take in his glorious riches. You will need a miracle from him so you can somehow know his love that surpasses knowledge. But rest assured, he wants you to be "filled to the measure of all the fullness of God"!

As you move into this third step, restoration, I urge you to learn to pray bold, faith-filled prayers. First, pray for the Spirit of wisdom and revelation, so you can know the Father better. Second, pray for your inner person to be strengthened so you can know the love that surpasses knowledge. These two father prayers offer you amazing, wonderful, life-changing news! Because of God's power and grace, each one of the four chambers of your heart can be filled.

17

LIFE-GIVING IDENTITY

Do these stories stir a hunger in your heart for a deeper connection with God as Father? I hope so, because that is what you were created for! Don't clean up your heart and then leave it empty. What has been cleansed needs to be filled.

When I walk with someone through the process of being refathered by God, we generally take the earliest defining moment the Counselor has brought to mind and work forward from there. After asking for the Spirit to show them what to cleanse from that memory (unforgiveness, sin, lies, idolatry, and vows—US LIV), I encourage them to respond with repentance and faith.

Either before these steps of cleansing, or after them, we pray the father prayers of Ephesians and ask for "the Spirit of wisdom and revelation." Specifically, we pray that God would reveal his father presence into that place so the person can receive his resources into their point of need. The Father loves to respond to this prayer, and he does so in many different ways. Sometimes the person and truth of Christ is revealed into a memory. Other times there are specific passages of Scripture, words from the Father, or a sense of his presence.

In each case I ask the person to stop and receive the presence of the Father. Connection with him touches every part of our being and centers us, recalibrating our souls as we become satisfied in him. It is important to stop and fully absorb this, because we know

God's father heart will be directed toward filling our core needs for identity, love, pleasure, and place.

Let's look at these four chambers of your heart again and see how they relate to each other. Notice the first two, identity and love, have to do more with "being"; and the second two, pleasure and place, with "doing." Sometimes people cast "being" and "doing" in contrast to each other, as if an increase in one requires the decrease in the other. "You need to do less and be more," they say, or "You need to stop just being and start doing something!" In Scripture, however, we find both closely connected, synergistically flowing out of and supporting each other.

There is also a special relationship between the chambers that sit diagonally across from each other. Identity and place are closely connected, like two sides of the same coin, since how God created you is designed to be expressed in your unique place in his big story. Love and pleasure are also closely connected, since one expresses the Father's commitment to you and the other his enjoyment in you. They are similar emotions, but they are distinguished by the fact that love is a decision and pleasure is a response.

Into all these chambers you need a constant stream of oxygenated blood, flowing from the Father, back to him, and out to others around you. A healthy heart pumps life-giving blood in a steady stream of giving and receiving, drawing off waste and poison, and sustaining your muscles and tissue with nutrition and life.

Now we will go deeper into how God wants to fill these four areas of your heart by looking at them one at a time. There is, however, a danger in this approach, because it might lead you to believe that the four chambers are separate from each other, when actually they are very closely connected.

The Father may concentrate on one of them for a time to bring it back to health, but he is always concerned and engaged with all four of these needs. As he reveals himself into the defining moments of your life, he will most likely deal with several of these core issues at the same time.

Let's take the first one and dig deeper into how the Father wants to fill your need for identity. As we look into Scripture, we find God addresses identity in both general and specific ways. If you are part of a soccer team, there is a common identity you share with your teammates as well as a specific identity that reflects the position you play on the field.

Because of the sacrifice of Jesus, those who believe in him have been adopted into God's family. This family inheritance gives us a powerful new common identity that should transform our lives. As Paul talks about the Christian's inheritance in the book of Ephesians, he uses words that describe not only what you have but also who you now are. What you can read in just fourteen verses about the amazing new nature you have in Christ should blow your mind. According to Ephesians 1:1–14, you are holy, blessed, chosen, blameless, loved, predestined, adopted, redeemed, forgiven, the object of God's grace, included, sealed with the Spirit, and God's possession.

Wow, that is astounding!

Does this make a difference in the way you view yourself and how you act? It should. A guilty man will hang his head in shame, looking down to avoid your eye and bracing himself for punishment. A forgiven man who has been made holy will hold his head high in honor, engaging without shame and moving forward without fear.

A woman who is left out and rejected will withdraw in pain, viewing herself as worthless and feeling she has nothing to give to others. A chosen woman who knows she is loved will be confident and radiant, knowing she belongs and secure in her place. From that safety and security, she will actively give and reach out to others.

When a seminary professor named Fred Craddock was vacationing in Tennessee, he sat down one evening with his wife for a quiet dinner in a restaurant near Gatlinburg. At least he expected the dinner would be quiet. Early in the meal an elderly man approached their table and begin to ask them questions.

"Where are you from," he bantered, "and what do you do for a living?" Put off by the old man's forward nature, and hoping to end the conversation, Craddock replied, "I'm a Christian minister." Somehow the old man didn't catch the hint, because he pulled up a chair and sat down after saying, "I owe a great deal to a minister of the Christian church." Then without further delay, the old man began to tell his story:

> I grew up in these mountains. My mother was not married, and the whole community knew it. I was what was called an illegitimate child. In those days that was a shame, and I was ashamed. . . . When I went into town with [my mother], I could see people staring at me, making guesses as to who was my father. At school the children said ugly things to me, and so I stayed to myself during recess, and I ate my lunch alone.
>
> In my early teens I began to attend a little church back in the mountains. . . . It had a minister who was both attractive and frightening. He had a chiseled face and a heavy beard and a deep voice. I went to hear him preach. I don't know exactly why, but it did something for me. However, I was afraid that I was not welcome since I was, as they put it, a bastard. So I would go just in time for the sermon, and when it was over I would move out because I was afraid that someone would say, "What's a boy like you doing in a church?"
>
> One Sunday some people queued up in the aisle before I could get out, and I was stopped. Before I could make my way through the group, I felt a hand on my shoulder, a heavy hand. It was that minister. . . . I trembled in fear. He turned his face around so he could see mine and seemed to be staring for a little

while. I knew what he was doing. He was going to make a guess as to who my father was. A moment later he said, "Well, boy, you're a child of . . ." and he paused there. And I knew it was coming. I knew I would have my feelings hurt. I knew I would not go back again. He said, "Boy, you're a child of God. I see a striking resemblance, boy." Then he swatted me on the bottom and said, "Now, you go claim your inheritance." I left the building a different person. In fact, that was really the beginning of my life.

The unexpected story was so moving that Craddock had to ask the old man's name. "Ben Hooper," he replied. It was only later that Craddock put the pieces together and realized that this very same Ben Hooper had been twice elected to serve as the governor of Tennessee.[12]

We discover *who* we are when we know *whose* we are. Did it make any difference to Ben Hooper to discover he was a child of God? Apparently discovering his identity made all the difference in the world! All true believers possess this new identity and receive this family inheritance. But the fact that we share this identity with others does nothing to dilute its potency. In addition, there is a unique role we play in God's family, a specific identity that is unlike any other.

Before you were conscious of life, Scripture tells us God was actively engaged in knitting you together in your mother's womb. Nothing was hidden from him in this secret place where you were "fearfully and wonderfully made" (Psalm 139:14). The psalmist recognized this careful creation led to a unique calling when he said, "Your eyes saw my unformed body; all the days ordained for me were written in your book before one of them came to be" (Psalm 139:16).

The particular way God created you gives you a unique package of weaknesses and strengths. The world we grow up in likes to measure and categorize us in a wide variety of ways. Endless competitions sort out who is the best in athletics, academics, beauty, performance, and achievement. Built into these systems is the presupposition that the person on top of the ladder has the most value and those farther down are less than ideal.

Others react to this system by trying to level the playing field. There is no winner, everyone gets an award, all of us are great, no matter what our performance. They do away with differences by insisting everyone is the same. This often leads to false confidence or condoned mediocrity.

In God's economy, neither of these is correct. Value comes from living out the unique identity he has created for you and excelling in the place he has specially prepared for you. It is a race, but one that is "marked out" for you rather than one where you try and steal the victory from someone else. You "run with perseverance," giving it your all, yet knowing yours is a path the Lord Jesus has uniquely given to you (Hebrews 12:1; see also Acts 20:24).

How do you feel about your particular collection of strengths and weaknesses? If you are like most people, there is a long list of things you would change if you could. Here are a few of mine: I wish I was more athletic; I wish I had a better memory; I wish my voice was more pleasing to the ear, like my wife's; I wish my face wasn't still pocked from teenage acne; I wish I wasn't so slow.

You may wish for a talent you don't have, a different kind of body, or an ability God has not given you. As you long for something different, you probably greatly underestimate the value of the strengths God wove into you. It can be easy to disregard these areas of strength because they seem easy to you—and thus inconsequential.

You can easily engage strangers in conversation, but that is no big deal. You can see the future with amazing clarity, but doesn't everyone? You have deep compassion and an amazing ability to serve, but what is that worth? We tend to long for what we don't have and minimize the value of what we do.

What if you truly believed that when God finished creating you, he stepped back and said with pride, "That is GOOD!" What if you were truly convinced that maximum value comes from living out what God specifically built into you, rather than longing for something else?

There is surprising wisdom and detail to the unique identity God has given you. When Amy Carmichael was a child in Northern Ireland, she possessed the only brown eyes in her family. Her mother had taught her to pray believing God would answer, so one night she asked God to change her eyes from brown to blue. Waking up the next morning, Amy ran to the mirror and immediately wailed in disappointment. It took her mother quite a while to convince Amy that no was also an answer from God.

Many years later, as Amy labored as a missionary in Bangalore, India, she heard of the plight of young girls dedicated to the pagan gods and given over to the temples. They served there as slaves, usually forced into prostitution to earn money for the priests. Even the Christians were against her when she entered the struggle to end the horrible service required of these little girls. In order to discover the truth, Amy dyed her skin darker and pretended to be Indian, entering the temples dressed in a sari. She could pass as a local Hindu woman only because her eyes were brown!

Amy went on to found the Dohnavur Fellowship, which became a sanctuary for over one thousand young children who would have otherwise spent their lives in temple slavery. When God knit Amy together in her mother's womb, he knew an unwanted characteristic like brown eyes would have great significance in his sovereign plan for her life.

Sometimes the gap between how God has made us and who we want to be is so great that we feel he must be cruel. Nick Vujicic was born with phocomelia, a rare condition characterized by the absence of limbs. Otherwise healthy, Nick literally had no arms and legs. As a child he watched his siblings run and pick up things, simple tasks he knew he would never do. Nick became angry at God and depressed, even attempting to drown himself in a bathtub and end his life.

Coming into a personal relationship with God through the leading and example of his parents, Nick finally came to terms with his condition and accepted the unique identity given to him by his Father. At seventeen, he founded a nonprofit organization called Life Without Limbs and began telling his story, encouraging people to overcome their limitations and find hope in Jesus Christ.

Since then untold numbers of people in over fifty countries of the world have heard his message. Scores of YouTube videos telling his story have been viewed millions of time. In each of these settings, Nick clearly points to the saving power of Christ. "It's been said that doors open to a man without arms and legs much more easily than to anyone else," he writes. "*We thank God for providing that privilege.* I've been invited into very unexpected places to share about my faith in Jesus Christ and literally millions have responded."[13]

Not long ago I saw a recording of Nick on *Oprah's Lifeclass* show. Overcome with tears at the power of his message, I found myself feeling another unexpected emotion—a longing for what Nick has. Of course, what Nick has is uniquely his. At first his condition seemed to be a mistake, but when he embraced it, he found his identity was full of the fingerprints of God. Your identity—and mine—carries that same unique and fabulous design.

You may need "the Spirit of wisdom and revelation" to fully see this with "the eyes of your heart" (Ephesians 1:17–18). You may need God to "strengthen you with power through his Spirit in your inner being" (Ephesians 3:16) so you can comprehend the full extent of his love for you. Are you asking the Father to do that? Are you listening as he speaks to you through his Spirit and through his Word?

Not long ago I experienced a stretch where I began to wander in my leadership. As Josiah Venture, the mission organization I lead, continued to grow, I found myself losing sight of who God wanted me to be in the midst of all the demands. I looked around me for strong leaders to model after and tried to catch some insight from them. I read some recent leadership books looking for new guiding principles. In spite of this, I found myself regularly pulled into the cracks of activities that were not particularly strategic. I could not see clearly who God wanted me to be.

Talking this over with my wife, she suggested a novel idea: "Why don't you go to the Father with that question?" That should have been obvious to me since I was regularly teaching on the fatherhood of God. Still, like you, sometimes I forget to apply what I know.

We set aside an evening to pray and seek God together. We reviewed the powerful truths God says about my identity because I belong to him. Then we asked him to show me more of how he has specifically created me to fulfill his will, the "race marked out" for me (Hebrews 12:1). We also asked if there were any defining moments he wanted to bring to mind through his Spirit, key memories into which he wanted to reveal his truth.

The Spirit took my thoughts back to an experience in high school when I attended a large youth conference with our denomination in the mountains of Colorado. In spite of the amazingly beautiful setting, it was a difficult week for me. I enjoyed the messages, but it seemed most of our group was not listening. The highlight for them was playing Rook way into the night and blinding people in the dark with a camera strobe. As much as I tried to join in, I felt out of sync and not part of the "gang." In high school, it's a big deal when you don't fit in.

During free time in the afternoons I would get on my bike, which I had somehow managed to cram in the back of our church van, and head up steep logging roads. The mountains fascinated me, and I wanted to get as high as possible. I loved seeing the big picture from some lofty vantage point and enjoyed fighting my way to the top of a hill where I could survey the entire valley and all the surrounding peaks.

Still, when I reached these stunning vistas and stopped to take them in, I felt alone. There was no one to share them with, no one else who wanted to spend their free time pedaling up some difficult mountain.

"Wow, I have no idea why you have taken me to this memory," I told the Lord in prayer. "Please show me what you want to reveal to me through your Spirit."

Then the Father began to speak to my heart.

There were no audible words. Yet all at once I understood that I had listened carefully to those conference messages because the Father had put a desire in my heart to serve him. That is part of how he had made me. I rode my bike up mountain roads because I enjoy difficult challenges that have meaning. The Father had created that enjoyment in me.

I saw for the first time that I loved getting up high because that is where I get the big picture. It is where I can see how things fit together and understand where the Father wants me to go. He had made me to love seeing the view from 10,000 feet so that I would have the ability to lead and inspire others.

Next I sensed my Father showing me why I had that lonely feeling at the top of the road. He doesn't want me to sweat my way up the hill on my own effort, pedaling in my own strength. The Father wants me to let him take me quickly up to altitude through his supernatural power and then fellowship there together with him. I am to take in the view beside my Father and let him show me what he sees and where he wants me to go. Then I can lead and inspire others with his strength and his inspiration.

The Spirit continued to show the Father's heart to me.

He took my thoughts to the group I was trying to get in with, and he showed me how distracting and unfulfilling it was to fight to fit in. What they were doing was the Father's responsibility, and I shouldn't judge their place from mine. Neither should I try to make a place somewhere with them, but rather find my place in him.

The Father's words to my spirit were strong and clear, breaking through my confusion with life-giving truth about my unique identity and place in his kingdom. With that came the nourishing power of his presence—the realization I was not alone. Those words of identity still help ground me today. I finished that time of prayer centered, satisfied, and wondering why it had taken me so many months to take this need to my limitless Father.

18

RELENTLESS LOVE

If you turn on the radio or scan the titles in a bookstore, you can't help but be struck by our culture's obsession with love. Love is the theme of countless stories, the focus of hundreds of movies, the engine behind billions of dollars of commerce. Covers of magazines announce the latest news about who has fallen in or out of love, and self-styled coaches line up to give us the latest tips on making love last. With all this information, we should be experts on love. I think we are just more confused. Into this chaos comes the voice of your Father, speaking strong but gentle words: "I love you." What exactly does that mean? We use the word *love* in so many different ways. I could say, "I love my wife," "I love my baby," "I love my biscuits dipped in gravy." Is the Father's love like any of those loves? Or is it different altogether?

I just finished paging through the fifty most popular love songs of all time, assembled by *Billboard* magazine on the basis of how long these songs spent at the top of the music charts. Scanning the titles was like a stroll through memory lane, since most of them have become embedded in our collective conscious, playing over and over again in the background of restaurants and shopping malls.

I saw "Love Story" by Taylor Swift; "She Loves You" by the Beatles; "I'll Make Love to You" by Boyz II Men; and "How Deep Is Your Love" by the Bee Gees. Taking position number 37 was Whitney Houston's power song about loving yourself, ironically titled "Greatest Love of All." At the very top of the list, in the number 1 slot was "Endless Love" by Diana Ross and Lionel Richie.

As I reflected on the lyrics to these culture-forming songs, two themes began to emerge. In many cases, the word *love* actually describes something taken from the other person rather than given. "I'll make love to you" sounds more like "I get to have sex with you." I make love, you become mine, and I love what I gain. Whitney encourages us to believe love directed toward yourself is actually the greatest love of all.

Does the Father have some hidden gain he is seeking when he says, "I love you"? Is he trying to take something from me or use the language of love to benefit himself? Is the Father seeking a feeling he wants to experience, a euphoria I am to generate for him? Does he need me to keep him emotionally warm and then softly leave, like the Bee Gees sing about in "How Deep Is Your Love"?

The Father's love is nothing like this. In fact, there are four unique characteristics of God's father love that are mind-blowing, radical, and in stark contrast to the frothy love that permeates pop culture.

The Father's love is preemptive

The Father always loves first. He loves us before we love him and before we have anything to merit his love. He loves us before we notice and before we respond. He loves when there is nothing lovely in us and no ability in us to give him anything in return. He loves first because his love is rooted in his own character—not in ours. Even our ability to desire his love and perceive his love comes because he first loved us.

"Here's the paradox," writes Ann Tatlock, award-winning author of the novel *All the Way Home*. "We can fully embrace God's love only when we recognize how completely unworthy of it we are."[14] The apostle John tells us, "This is love: not that we loved God, but that he loved us" (1 John 4:10). Paul wrote, "God demonstrates his own love for us in this: While we were still sinners, Christ died for us" (Romans 5:8). Frederick Buechner, in his book *The Magnificent Defeat*, tried to explain it this way:

> We are children, perhaps, at the very moment when we know that it is as children that God loves us—not because we have deserved his love and not in spite of our undeserving; not because we try and not because we recognize the futility of our trying; but simply because he has chosen to love us. We are children because he is our father; and all of our efforts, fruitful and fruitless, to do good, to speak truth, to understand, are the efforts of children who, for all their precocity, are children still in that before we loved him, he loved us, as children, through Jesus Christ our lord.[15]

The Father's love is sacrificial

Love is easy when the music is low and the emotions are high. But love that expresses itself in blood, sweat, and tears is love of another kind. By his actions the Father showed his willingness to sacrifice on our behalf. When our sin escalated the cost of love to the very highest price, the Father paid it with the blood of his one and only Son.

Christ's death should convince us there is no boundary to the sacrificial love of the Father. That is why Paul said, "If God is for us, who can be against us? He who did not spare his own Son, but gave him up for us all—how will he not also, along with him, graciously give us all things?" (Romans 8:31–32).

Often we have an internal sense of reciprocity. We ask for help from others only when we know we can give them something in return. We don't want to overextend our welcome, be too much of a bother, or expect too much. Somehow we sense there is a bank account that could be overdrawn, a credit limit we dare not pass, a level of receiving that appropriately reflects what we have earned or deserved.

A commitment to reciprocity and fairness will firmly block your ability to receive the Father's love, since your credit is depleted in an instant. The Father is always drawing off his bank account, not yours, always giving off his credit, not your merit, always granting you gifts you could never repay. Each time he loves you, it costs him something. Selfless love makes him willing to pay that price.

The Father's love is incomprehensible

God *is* love. Every other love is a derivative, a smaller version of the love he possesses. Our categories will never be large enough to map out his love; our understanding will never be capable of comprehending its depths. That is why Paul prays that we might "know this love that surpasses knowledge" (Ephesians 3:19) and declares "we are more than conquerors" (Romans 8:37), since nothing, "in all creation, will be able to separate us from the love of God" (Romans 8:39). C. S. Lewis put it this way:

> In awful and surprising truth, we are the objects of His love. You asked for a loving God: you have one. The great spirit you so lightly invoked, the 'lord of terrible aspect', is present: not a senile benevolence that drowsily wishes you to be happy in your own way, not the cold philanthropy of a conscientious magistrate, nor the care of a host who feels responsible for the comfort of his guests, but the consuming fire Himself, the Love that made the worlds, persistent as the artist's love for his work and despotic as a man's love for a dog, provident and venerable as a father's love for a child, jealous, inexorable, exacting as love

between the sexes. . . . It is certainly a burden of glory not only beyond our deserts but also, except in rare moments of grace, beyond our desiring.[16]

The vast nature of God's capacity means you will never finish expanding your understanding and experience of the Father's love. It is always bigger than you see, always deeper than you feel, always more real than you experience and more wonderful than you imagine. "We should be astonished at the goodness of God," wrote author Brennan Manning, "stunned that He should bother to call us by name, our mouths wide open at His love, bewildered that at this very moment we are standing on holy ground."[17]

The Father's love is completely good

One of the top fifty love songs on the *Billboard* list actually questions the value of love. "What's love got to do with it?" belts Tina Turner. "What's love but a secondhand emotion." As the beat drives on, we discover why Turner is so nervous about giving in to love: "Who needs a heart when a heart can be broken?" she cries.

At the bridge, Tina's complaint becomes even clearer. "I've been taking on a new direction. But I have to say, I've been thinking about my own protection. It scares me to feel this way." Why is love scary? Why is Turner thinking about her own protection? Because love makes us uniquely vulnerable. The betrayal of love can cause debilitating pain. Most of us know this from personal experience, and our past disappointments create a basic posture of self-protection. It is better to be a bit aloof, a bit skeptical, a bit held back when someone expresses love toward us. Better to be safe now than sorry later.

Perhaps this is logical when it comes to people, but it is dangerous when it comes to God. Questioning the goodness of the Father's love created a willful distance in Eve that produced the original, creation-crushing sin. As Martin Luther once said, "The sin underneath all our sins is to trust the lie of the serpent that we cannot trust the love and grace of Christ and must take matters into our own hands."[18]

There is no other love that is completely untainted and utterly pure. Our earthly experiences of love can lead us to a partial embrace of God's love, a skeptical, aloof stance that is "thinking about my own protection." The Father's love is unlike any other love. It is COMPLETELY good. In fact, his love creates the greatest protection you could ever find—far better than any safety you could try to cobble together on your own.

There is one characteristic of the top fifty love songs that you *will* find in God's love. All these popular songs speak to an emotion experienced when love is received, an impact love makes that is intuitive and difficult to explain. Although God's love is incomprehensibly greater than this romantic love, it does not exist like some special gem in a museum, enclosed in glass and isolated from our touch. We do not just contemplate the matchless love of God from afar. We emotionally and intuitively experience the love of the Father up close, in a very personal way.

The evangelist D. L. Moody wrote of times when he was so overwhelmed by the love of God that he had to "ask Him to stay His hand."[19] Desmond Tutu tried to describe this intuitive experience of God's love by saying it is "like when you sit in front of a fire in winter—you are just there in front of the fire. You don't have to be smart or anything. The fire warms you."[20]

When I lead people through the process of being re-fathered by God, there are often particular moments where the Father reveals his love to them. Often they express this with descriptions like, "I feel the Father's arms around me," or "I'm sitting in the Father's lap with my head buried in his chest," or "I feel his strong hand on my shoulder." When I ask them to tell me more, they often say, "It's the best feeling in the whole world."

When I ask, "What do you feel when you let yourself receive the Father's love?" almost always the answer is the same: "I feel safe."

In an "Open Letter to Family Men," published in *Our Daily Bread,* author Linda Anderson describes watching her daughter experience the love of her dad: "She was blond and beautiful, with azure eyes and a tumble of tawny curls. At three years of age, she would climb into her daddy's lap, snuggle up with a wide, satisfied smile, and purr, 'This is my safe place!' And so it was."[21]

You and I are grown now, but we still need a "safe place." That place can only be found in the arms of our heavenly Father, as we rest in his limitless love. God wants you to be "rooted and established" in this love (Ephesians 3:17). And you need it more than you know.

The Father's love is YOUR safe place.

19

GODLY PLEASURE

Aria Shahrokhshahi struggled with the demands of math in his British prep school. After receiving an F in the September marking season, he knew his poor performance created a very serious situation. If he couldn't pull up his grade by the end of fall semester, it would be difficult, if not impossible, to gain a spot in the university. January marking season came, and Aria braced himself for the news. His teacher handed him the results. Cautiously opening the envelope, Aria read the grade report—and broke down in tears. He had brought his score up from an F to a C.

His thoughts immediately went to his dad, Farhnoosh, and how he would respond. Back at home, waiting for his dad to get home from work, Aria came up with a plan to capture his dad's reaction on video. Setting up his computer in the corner of the kitchen, Aria waited for the sound of the key in the front door. Hearing his father arrive, he started the camera on this computer, and then he called out to his dad.

"Dad, I need to you come here. I've got something from school and I need you to look at it. It's really important." The hidden camera caught Aria pacing and looking around the room nervously as he waited for his dad to come in, then holding the door open with his foot to clear the way. Still wearing an overcoat, looking at the floor, his mind obviously full of cares from the day, Farhnoosh started through the door. Before he could fully enter the kitchen,

Aria handed him the note from school. Farhnoosh read it slowly, turning it over several times in his hands as Aria watched him intently.

Glancing up suddenly from the paper, Farhnoosh looked his son in the eye for the first time since he came in. "Is that real?" he asked.

"Yes," Aria responded tentatively.

Immediately Farhnoosh asked the same question again, almost yelling with excitement. "Is that real?"

"Yes," Aria replied, his voice rising to match his father's intensity.

"Oh m-y-y-y-y!" Farhnoosh cried. His words were punctuated by sobs as he became overcome with emotion. Shaking as he cried, he embraced his son, so full of joy he could hardly catch his breath.

"Are you sure?" He asked again, pulling back from his embrace to look Aria in the face. "Yes," Aria responded, and Farhnoosh launched into another round of sobs that sounded like a mixture of crying and laughing.

Wiping the tears from his eyes, Farhnoosh looked at the paper again. "I can't believe it. So you don't need to take it again?" Aria nodded.

"You're set for life," Farhnoosh said, and Aria broke out in laughter at the obvious overstatement, yet basked in his father's approval at the same time. "You're set for life," Farhnoosh said again.[22]

"I knew how he would react," Aria later explained. "He's a very emotional guy. I just didn't know he was going to be that loud and emotional. It was a little bit crazy."

Aria kept his precious recording to himself for almost a year, and then decided to post it on YouTube under the title "The Day I Passed Maths." The video immediately went viral, racking up 1.5 million views in just two weeks. *TODAY News* picked up the story and arranged a live interview with Aria and his dad.

"Basically, Aria has always found math difficult," Farhnoosh said, as the interviewers probed to discover why he reacted so enthusiastically to what was still a rather low grade. "To go from an F to a C is a huge jump. It's the same as going from a C to an A-star. I was just overwhelmed, absolutely overwhelmed."

"Everyone is so nice on all the comments," Aria said, flashing a beaming smile toward his dad. "Everyone's congratulating me, I've been getting tweets, and everyone has been saying how much of a good father I've got. It was a very important moment in my life. I thought, why not share one of the happiest moments in my life with the world, so that's why I just put it on."[23]

What made this one of the happiest moments in Aria's life? Because he had just received a full dose of his father's pleasure. Why did his video resonate with millions of people all over the world? Because all of us long for the same.

Today, well over five million people have watched Aria's simple video.[24]

Of course, you may have experienced something entirely different in your home. In his men's seminar, David Simmons, a former cornerback for the Dallas Cowboys, tells about his upbringing. His father, a military man, was extremely demanding, rarely saying a kind word, always pushing him with harsh criticism to do better. When Dave played football in high school, his father was unrelenting in his criticisms. "Most boys got butterflies in the stomach before the game; I got them afterwards. Facing my father was more stressful than facing any opposing team."

He chose to play football at the University of Georgia because its campus was farther from home than any school that offered him a scholarship. After college, he became the second-round draft pick of the St. Louis Cardinals professional football club. Joe Namath (who later signed with the New York Jets), was the club's first-round pick that year. Excited, Simmons telephoned his father to tell him the good news.

"How does it feel to be second?" his dad said.[25] Ouch!

Our hearts were designed to experience the pleasure and delight of a father. A father's delight motivates us and gives us healthy confidence and energy. It makes sacrifice and effort worthwhile. What can we expect as we come to our heavenly Father? Since he is perfect, is his standard so high we can never achieve it? Since he has other children, is he comparing our performance to theirs, asking us how it feels to be "second"?

There are two common misunderstandings of the Father's pleasure—first, that he is never pleased; and second, that he is always pleased. Part of God's pleasure comes from what he has done to adopt us into his family. Ephesians tells us, "In love he predestined us for adoption to sonship through Jesus Christ, *in accordance with his pleasure* and will" (1:4–5, emphasis added). Paul went on to write, "With all wisdom and understanding, he made known to us the mystery of his will *according to his good pleasure*" (Ephesians 1:8–9, emphasis added).

In other words, when the Father looks at you, he experiences great pleasure in what *he* has done. He chose you, he redeemed you, he revealed himself to you, he made you holy, and he made you his child. This brings him deep joy.

Parents experience this same delight as they look at their newborn babies and beam with pride, even though their babies can only look back up at them with a bewildered gaze as they lay helplessly on their backs, unable to even lift their heads. The parents' joy has nothing to do with their baby's performance, nothing to do with ranking or accomplishments. Their newborn brings great pleasure just by his or her presence, and great joy because he or she belongs to them.

Babies sense this joy and feed off it, waiting for the moment they can catch their parents' eyes, and grinning in anticipation of the expression of delight they will see. The joy of pleasing our father or mother is one of the first emotions we experience as a small child. Do you anticipate a flash of delight as you catch your heavenly Father's eyes and see his response of joy because you belong to him and he has made you his child?

In Zephaniah 3:17 the prophet tells us, "The LORD your God is *with you*, the Mighty Warrior who saves. He will take *great delight* in you; in his love he will no longer rebuke you, but will *rejoice over you with singing*" (emphasis added).

Can you imagine the God of the universe, your Father, taking such great delight in you that he rejoices over you with singing? Amazing! Do you still feel deep down inside of you a sense that the Father is never pleased with you? If you are his child, that feeling does not reflect reality. His delight in you begins with his performance, not yours.

At the same time, there is an aspect of his pleasure that *is* based on how you live and what you do. "But my righteous one will live by faith. And I take *no pleasure* in the one who shrinks back" (Hebrews 10:38, emphasis added). Paul assured the believers in Ephesus of the position they had in Christ and then urged them to lives worthy of that calling: "For you were once darkness, but now you are light in the Lord. Live as children of light (for the fruit of the light consists in all goodness, righteousness and truth) and *find out what pleases the Lord*" (Ephesians 5:8–10, emphasis added).

The delight Farhnoosh expressed toward Aria had significance because it was a genuine response to true effort. Reward has no meaning if no effort is required to obtain it. This desire to please the Father energized the direction and focus of Paul's life. "So *we make it our goal to please him*," he wrote, "whether we are at home in the body or away from it. For we must all appear before the judgment seat of Christ, so that each of us may receive what is due us for the things done while in the body, whether good or bad" (2 Corinthians 5:9–10, emphasis added).

Sometimes, in our relief that Jesus took the burden of our punishment, we forget we will still face the judgment seat of Christ to determine our reward. Our works on earth will be evaluated to see if they are good or bad. Some of us will receive a prize and hear the amazing words "Well done" from the Father. Others will be saved but receive nothing more, entering heaven "only as one escaping through the flames" (1 Corinthians 3:15).

So, what exactly does the Father delight in? You and I desperately need to know the answer to this question.

You need to invest energy in finding out what pleases God, because it is often very different from what you would expect. If we project our own aspirations on the Father, or assume he is simply a voice for the expectations of people around us, we could wander far off track, or give up altogether.

Out of all the things we could possibly do, what would please our Father the very most? The list is not long. It is not impossible. His expectations are not hidden, nor do they change. The Father is most pleased by four things.

Faith

Over and over again in Scripture, God tells us how much the Father values faith. Regarding those who are caught in the trap of religious ritual yet lacking a living faith, God says, "But my righteous one will live by faith" (Hebrews 10:38). The writer of Hebrews goes on to argue that "without faith it is *impossible to please God*, because anyone who comes to him must believe that he exists and that he rewards those who earnestly seek him" (Hebrews 11:6, emphasis added).

This should be a great encouragement to us, because faith is something we can exercise in any circumstance. We can express faith at all times, in every kind of condition. Faith is always possible, always accessible, and always under my control. I can choose to believe when I'm in the dark valley or on the mountaintop. I can exercise faith in prison or in positions of great prestige. I can believe what God says and act on it when I am weak and incompetent, and when I am strong and capable.

Faith can be expressed in the small things that fill our every day or in courageous actions that have historic significance. I can believe in the midst of tremendous knowledge or with the simple ignorance of a child. Every time I believe God and act on the basis of that belief, I can be sure the Father is pleased. I can turn my eyes toward his and catch the joy of his delight. Not only is he pleased, but he actively rewards those who earnestly seek him.

Obedience

Someone once said, "Obedience is God's love language." It brings the Father great delight when he sees you listening to his voice and doing what he says. When confronted with Saul's self-justified explanation as to why he hadn't kept God's instructions, Samuel said, "Does the LORD delight in burnt offerings and sacrifices as much as in obeying the LORD? To obey is better than sacrifice, and to heed is better than the fat of rams" (1 Samuel 15:22).

It might seem self-serving for the Father to delight in our obedience, but the opposite is true. When we obey, we actually do what is best for us, since his commands are always designed to bless us and lead us into abundant life. When we obey, we draw close to him as we join his path, rather than pushing him away as we pridefully make our own way. This close fellowship makes him glad. When we obey, we demonstrate our trust in him, which brings him great joy.

Remember that obedience is not just intellectual agreement but responsive action. Just acknowledging, "Yeah, yeah, you are right," is not the same as stopping whatever you are doing and putting into action what the Father says. Delayed obedience is disobedience. The Father is pleased by your quick response.

Submission

In some situations, there is no specific step of obedience that is needed but rather the willing act of coming under the Father's authority, a humbling of yourself and an acknowledgment that he is your Lord. Any time you actively place yourself in the right posture of submission to the Father, it pleases him.

David put it this way: "You do not *delight* in sacrifice, or I would bring it; you do not *take pleasure* in burnt offerings. My sacrifice, O God, is a broken spirit; a broken and contrite heart you, God, will not despise" (Psalm 51:16–17, emphasis added).

If you are a father or mother, think about how much joy it brings you when your child submits to your leadership, or asks for forgiveness when they have done wrong, or lets you know they will bend their will to yours. You are immediately proud of them and delighted by the fact that you can now direct them in the way that is best. It brings you great joy when they willingly put themselves into a proper place of submission to you as their parent, when they don't pretend they have all the answers or know what is best. In the same way, when you say to your heavenly Father "Not my will, but your will be done," you can be sure he is very pleased.

Service

The Father always invites you into his work—but not because he cannot manage all his responsibilities on his own or accomplish all his purposes without your help. If his power could create the universe with merely a spoken word, he can easily achieve his objectives without your assistance. In spite of this, the Father invites you to join him in his work as a son or daughter and as an heir. His invitation to serve is a blessing to be embraced, a privilege to be entered into.

When you accept his invitation and join the Father in what he is doing, it brings him joy. In spite of the fact that Paul's assignment was filled with hardship and difficulty, he considered it a very high calling. "Join with me in suffering," he wrote, "like a good soldier of Christ Jesus. No one serving as a soldier gets entangled in civilian affairs, *but rather tries to please* his commanding officer" (2 Timothy 2:3–4, emphasis added).

This single-minded focus of serving his Father and joining the Father's work energized every act Jesus did on earth. "When you have lifted up the Son of Man," Jesus said, "then you will know that I am he and that I do nothing on my own but speak just what the Father has taught me. The one who sent me is with me; he has not left me alone, for *I always do what pleases him*" (John 8:28–29, emphasis added).

Serving the Father will often express itself in service to others. However, it is important to always keep in mind exactly who you are striving to please. Trying to satisfy others will leave you empty and burned out, since there will always be more needs than you can possibly meet. Serving your Father, who is inviting you into his work and coordinating all the other pieces that need to be brought to bear, is something altogether different.

Look again at the top four things on the Father's list: *faith, obedience, submission,* and *service*. Are these possible? Are these rewards that could be attained? When you do any of these four things, it brings the Father joy. His delight and pleasure should touch you deeply. Just like Aria, these experiences of feeling his pleasure can be some of the "happiest moments" of your life.

If you try to please the Father AND everyone else, you certainly won't win the honor of hearing his words "Well done." In your attempt to gain others' approval, you will lose the approval that means the very most. As you scan the crowd of people looking on, you have to have eyes for just One. The rest of the voices need to fade into the background as you seek the pleasure of the only One whose opinion really matters—your Father.

Eric Liddell, often called the "Flying Scotsman," was born on January 16, 1902, in Tianjin, northern China, to Rev. and Mrs. James Dunlop Liddell, who were Scottish missionaries with the London Missionary Society. Moving back to Scotland to attend school, Liddell excelled in every kind of sport, but he showed particular promise in track and field. While continuing his studies at Oxford, he became known as the fastest runner in Scotland, and many began to speculate that he was their best hope for the Olympic Games.

Liddell's commitment to God affected every area of his life, and though he was preparing for mission work in China, he saw his running as part of his service to God. In the famous movie based on his life, *Chariots of Fire*, Liddell is quoted to say, "I believe God made me for a purpose, but he also made me fast. And when I run I feel his pleasure." Chosen to represent his country in the 1924 Olympic Games, Eric received word that the 100 meter, his strongest race, was scheduled to be run on Sunday. Immediately Liddell sent his reply: "I'm not running."

Disappointed, but left without much choice, his team assigned him the much longer 400-meter distance, which fell on a different day. Just before the race began, an American team masseur handed Liddell a piece of paper with the following words from 1 Samuel 2:30: "Those who honor me I will honor." Liddell ran the entire race holding on to that piece of paper. He won the race in 47.6 seconds, shattering the existing world record.

Eric Liddell lived every area of his life out of an energy focused on pleasing his heavenly Father. This gave him unusual humility and motivated him to great accomplishments. People everywhere liked him, in part because he seemed to not need their praise. *"Entirely without vanity, he was enormously popular,"* said his headmaster at Eltham College, George Robertson. *"Very early he showed signs of real character. . . . There was no pride or fuss about him, but he knew what he stood for."*[26]

A writer for the Edinburgh University newspaper, *The Student*, made the following observation: "Ninety-nine men, gifted with Eric's prowess, would now be insufferably swollen headed, but here we have the hundredth man. Here is a man who hates praise and shuns publicity, yet is deserving of both. . . . Everyone is fond of Eric."[27] *The Scotsman* paper, on July 19, 1924, reported on the speech Liddell made after winning the gold:

> The shouting and the cheering suddenly ceased, and he began to speak. The modesty and simplicity and directness of his words went straight to the heart. No adulation, no fame, no flattery can ever affect this youth. . . . He made us quickly realize that running was not to be his career. He was training to be a missionary in China, and he was to devote all his spare time until he set forth for the East in evangelistic work among the young men in Scotland. And he asked for our help. What a hush suddenly fell. The Olympic Games were forgotten; the olive crowns and the thunder of cheers; and we saw this young man go forth on his mission. . . . It is because he has mastered himself, and has guided his course by the eternal stars, that Eric

Liddell came to that laurel crown. He is running a race, and he
will stay it even to the end.[28]

Eric died as a missionary martyr imprisoned in a Japanese
prison camp in China in 1945. But he lived with a clarity and
energy that comes from pleasing an audience of one. This enabled
him to run the race faithfully to the very end. Now he is experiencing his Father's delight firsthand—forever.

20

A PLACE OF YOUR OWN

Our need for *place* wells up from the very core of who we are as human beings.

God's first act in relationship to the first man and woman was to give them a place in his creation and a place in his purposes. Immediately after God created Adam and Eve, he put them in the Garden of Eden to work it and take care of it. Part of the Father's dominion was entrusted to them, and they were given authority to exercise leadership and act on his behalf in that place.

When God gave Adam and Eve instructions about their stewardship, he marked out clear boundaries and gave them a surprising level of ownership and authority within those boundaries: "God blessed them and said to them, *'Be fruitful and increase* in number; *fill the earth* and subdue it. *Rule over* the fish in the sea and the birds in the sky and over every living creature that moves on the ground.' Then God said, *'I give you* every seed-bearing plant on the face of the whole earth and every tree that has fruit with seed in it. *They will be yours* for food' " (Genesis 1:28–29, emphasis added).

This gift of place gave Adam and Eve direction and purpose. It gave them resources and ownership under the lordship of the Father. Their gift of place was a blessing because "God blessed them." The Father's key role in blessing his children looms large in the lives of the early patriarchs. When Abraham, Jacob, or Joseph laid hands on their children's heads and blessed them, the words they spoke gave each child a unique gift of identity and place.

Remember we observed how closely these two gifts relate to each other, like two sides of the same coin? Receiving the father's blessing empowered the next generation with a clear sense of who they were and what they were to do. It marked out clear territory and gave them confidence and direction to engage in their calling.

Take a quick look around you, and you will see this need for place expressed in so many ways. Why is ownership of land, ideas, and possessions so important to us? Why do we long for clear positions or important titles? Why do fashions and styles need to change so it is obvious that our generation and time are distinct and different from the last?

Why are we so drawn to stories like those in *The Lord of the Rings* or *Harry Potter* series, where an ordinary character suddenly discovers he or she has a special call, a "chosen" destiny? Why do we desire to be unique, unusual, distinct, or different? Why do we long to make our mark, do something significant, or make a difference?

I believe all these desires spring from our God-given longing for place. This need can and should be filled by the Father. If it is not, we will either try to fill it in other ways, or we will become deadened, without purpose and without direction. Without knowing your place, you will not know what you are supposed to do.

Phil Vischer started Big Idea Productions in a spare bedroom with a small loan from a sympathetic Bible study friend. In 1993 his small team produced the first VeggieTales episode, "Where's God When I'm S-Scared?" The unique vegetable characters, chosen because their simple shapes could be produced by first-generation animation software, quickly became a hit with families across the United States. Soon children everywhere knew the struggles of Bob the Tomato and could sing silly songs with Larry the Cucumber.

Over the next ten years VeggieTales sold more than 25 million videos. The company grew to 210 employees, poaching talent from major studios, and even producing a major motion picture called *Jonah*. The full-length feature earned $24 million at the box office and sold three million copies, but even that success was not enough to sustain the company's rapid growth.

In 2003 Big Idea went into bankruptcy. Vischer lost everything. He described it this way: "It was about six years of going up very quickly, then about three to four years that I have described to people as falling down a flight of stairs in slow motion."

"As Big Idea grew, Vischer began to craft a master plan for its future," wrote Bob Smietana, who interviewed Vischer shortly after the company's collapse. "He saw two possibilities. He could remain a storyteller like C. S. Lewis, or he could become an 'empire builder,' like another of his heroes, Walt Disney. Being the next Walt Disney also felt a lot better than being plain old Phil. A middle child, whose dad left home when he was nine, Vischer felt invisible as a kid. His drive to build Big Idea—a company whose positive messages would strengthen families—was fueled by his childhood experience of loss."

"When the first VeggieTales video started to catch on," Vischer said, "I remember my sister saying, 'We never thought you'd amount to much'—which was partly joking, but only partly. I really felt driven, I think, to prove that I actually existed. The bigger it got, the more I felt validated. I am not nobody—I am Mr. Big Idea guy. I was trying to be someone that God didn't call me to be and that God didn't create me to be," he continued. "It wasn't working, and I couldn't see a way out without disappointing a lot of people. So I kept beating my head against the Walt door, trying to get in."

Several months after the bankruptcy, the wife of a Big Idea artist wrote an e-mail to Vischer. While praying for him, a powerful and vivid image had entered her mind. She wrote, "I saw you at Disneyland, and you were looking for your father and you couldn't find him."[29]

How many of us are still looking for our Father but not able to find him? The contemporary poet Diane Wakoski captured some of the heartbreak of this search in her very personal poem, "The Father of My Country." An excerpt from this poem appears below:

> *other children said, "My father is a doctor,"*
> *or*
> *"My father gave me this camera,"*
> *or*
> *"My father took me to*
> *the movies,"*
> *or*
> *"My father and I went swimming,"*
> *but*
> *. . .*
> *my father was not in the telephone book*
> *in my city;*
> *my father was not sleeping with my mother*
> *at home;*
> *my father did not care if I studied the*
> *piano;*
> *my father did not care what*
> *I did;*
> *and I thought my father was handsome and I loved him and I wondered*
> *why*
> *he left me alone so much,*
> *so many years*
> *in fact, but*

my father made me what I am,
a lonely woman,
without a purpose, just as I was
a lonely child
without any father. I walked with words, words, and names,
names. Father was not
one of my words.
Father was not
one of my names. [30]

I feel speechless with loss every time I read this poem. You may know this loss personally, and if you told your stories to Diane or Phil, they would nod with understanding. In spite of that, I have good news for you. You are not a slave to the failures of your father. If you had an engaged father, who did a good job of passing on a blessing, I have good news for you too. You have a heavenly Father who has prepared and is preparing a place for you. His gift of place is much better than the best efforts your earthly father could provide.

Most people are familiar with the conversation Jesus had with his disciples in the upper room when he revealed he was going to heaven to prepare a place for them. In John 14:2 we read this promise of Jesus: "My Father's house has many rooms." Jesus was assuring the disciples that the Father had set aside a unique part of heaven for each of them.

Can you imagine that? Even in heaven you are not anonymous and lost in the masses. You have a unique place given by the Father! I wonder how that room is decorated, or what furniture he has placed there in advance. To be sure, it is perfectly tailored to reflect your unique character and nature. When you arrive there, you will feel more "at home" than you ever have felt in your life.

The Bible tells us that heaven will also include stewardship positions that have been given to us and responsibilities entrusted to us—cities that some will rule over. If heaven is a restoration of God's original design, we certainly must expect it would include a perfect gift of place that is similar to what Adam and Eve experienced in the garden. Each of us will have a call and a purpose.

But we don't have to wait for heaven to enjoy the blessing of place from the Father. In fact, he began preparing your place before you were born, and he begins to give you your inheritance the moment you put your trust in him. Paul tells us that we are his workmanship, "created in Christ Jesus to do good works, which God *prepared in advance for us to do*" (Ephesians 2:10, emphasis added).

You have a call, a purpose, a unique part of God's possession entrusted to you. It perfectly matches who you are, because you are his workmanship. You don't have to somehow assemble it from nothing, because it is already prepared in advance. Your responsibility is to receive this wonderful series of good works that is uniquely yours, and walk in them.

The psalmist wrote, "All the days ordained for me were written in your book before one of them came to be" (Psalm 139:16). What a joy to know that my Father is thinking ahead, opening the way, entrusting a place in his kingdom to me, and then personally taking responsibility for defending it and making it secure. This is the confidence David spoke of when he wrote: "LORD, you alone are my portion and my cup; you make my lot secure. The boundary lines have fallen for me in pleasant places; surely I have a delightful inheritance" (Psalm 16:5–6).

Do you realize what it means to have an inheritance when your Father is the King? It means you don't have to fight for your place or shove someone over to make space for you. You don't have to push someone else down so you can move up. It means you don't have to prove yourself, or make a name for yourself, or pridefully promote yourself. The Lord is your portion and your cup.

Since he makes your lot secure, you don't have to feel threatened by attacks, or panicked about the future, or anxious about what you could lose. You have a Defender, you have an Advocate, you have a Protector who will take up your case. You can rejoice with the successes of others, since their blessings are not a threat to yours. You can lean forward into the responsibilities the Father has entrusted to you, because you know he has prepared both you and them. You can enjoy the journey, because the path has been scouted out ahead. Instead of chasing the illusion that the grass is greener on other side of the fence, you can soak in the fact that your boundary lines have fallen in "pleasant places."

You can rest in the assurance that your place has been given to you. You are not a squatter who is hoping no one will kick you out. You are not couch surfing; you are not bumming a ride. You are a legitimate son or daughter, not an impostor.

Surely you have a "delightful inheritance."

If this is true, doesn't it make sense to run to the Father for his instructions whenever you are unclear about your place? If you act like an orphan, you might get way off track trying to be adopted by someone else. Just like Phil, your version of "Walt" might take you to a place that God has not entrusted to you and cause you to lose the inheritance that is actually yours.

This is idolatry, one of the five diseases of the heart that must be cleansed to make space for the Father. For Vischer, that meant a trip to Disneyland to make his peace with Walt Disney—or at least with his statue. "I am done now," Vischer said. "You can be you, and I will be me."[31]

In order to seek your place from the only One who can truly give you place, you need to stop and listen, asking the questions that are on your heart and waiting in faith for his answer. Look at all the different ways the Father communicated with his sons and daughters in the stories we have recorded in Scripture. He was relentless and persistent in telling his children what he had prepared for them and how they could walk in his path. Don't you think he would do the same for you, oh you of little faith?

Like you, I need to be reminded that God really is my Father, and he really has prepared my place. I often need the "eyes of my heart enlightened" and "the Spirit of wisdom and revelation" to go beyond just theological conviction to an experienced reality.

For example, about ten years ago in our work in Eastern Europe, God began to lead us through a period of innovation into new kinds of ministry we had never experienced before—opportunities with media, open doors into public schools, new countries with cultures that were confusing to me. While it was all very exciting, I felt like I had somehow snuck into an important meeting without a badge, or ended up in a role for which I had no qualifications. At any moment someone would surely find out I really didn't belong here and kick me out.

A portion of my energy every day was lost to nervousness, as I braced myself for the potential sudden loss of place. I deeply enjoyed what God had entrusted to us, which made me even more concerned it would somehow slip out of my hands. This made me overreact to criticism and invest much energy in self-defense. Rather than openly stewarding the responsibilities I had, I was clutching them tightly, hoping no one would take them away.

Knowing my spirit was not in the right place, I asked my wife, Connie, to join me in a time of seeking the Father's voice. We arranged for someone to watch the kids, and we set aside the better part of a day to seek God and listen to him.

After sharing more of what was going on in my heart with Connie, and hearing her observations and thoughts, we asked the Counselor to give us his insights. The Holy Spirit showed me that I was wearing a patchwork cloak, one I had sewn together from scraps collected on my own. I longed to have a mantle entrusted from God but somehow assumed it was up to me to put that together.

So I looked around me for others who had a God-given cloak and tried to borrow a piece of their blessing. If I could grab a bit of D. L. Moody, a scrap from Hudson Taylor, a piece of my mentor, Rich Kerns, and a couple of buttons from *Christianity Today* to hold it all together, I might have the authority to act on God's behalf. However, the cloak was ill fitting and obviously poorly sewn. It didn't cover me properly, and I sensed the pieces belonged to someone else and not to me.

I remembered how I had sat in church as a young child and read the bulletin inserts, each week featuring another story of a great man or woman of God. I longed to be included in that list someday, so I would daydream during the sermon, fantasizing what they might one day write about me. However, those great stories were my own creation, compiled from the journeys of others, rather than received from my loving Father.

I asked the Spirit what I was to do with my patchwork cloak. He told me to take it off and destroy it. It was my creation, my design, not a cloak given to me by him. This felt terrifying to me. Without the cloak I would be truly adrift, without authority to act, and without a position to serve from. My worst fears would be realized. Only by a sheer act of the will did I proceed forward with obedience, because everything in me was screaming to protect the place I had made. Forcing out words of repentance with a trembling heart, I took off and destroyed the coat I had made and turned to the Father with empty hands, fearful there would be nothing to receive.

Connie and I waited in silence for the Father to speak. Then my body began to shake with sobs. I'm not an overly emotional person, and Connie had never seen me cry like this before. She looked up with a fearful expression on her face and asked me what was wrong. Her eyes grew wider with concern when she realized I was sobbing so hard I couldn't even speak. "Are you all right, Dave?" she asked, putting her hand on my shoulder and trying to make sense of my response.

I was gasping for air. "He . . . gave . . . me . . . my . . . cloak," I blurted out between sobs, overcome by emotion and barely able to speak. It wasn't until several moments later that I could say more. "It is a beautiful cloak," I told Connie, "made with thick, sturdy material, tailored perfectly to my frame. It covers me completely, yet moves so fluidly as I walk or act on his behalf. It is given by the Father and carries his seal of authority, his mark of quality, his designation of purpose. The moment I put it on I feel two wonderful emotions—great purpose and tremendous rest."

The next day I engaged in many of the same responsibilities, but they all felt so different. I experienced joy and safety rather than fear and dread, anticipation rather than nervousness, a clear sense of purpose and direction rather than a feeling of being alone in the dark. I knew that the Father had given me my portion and my cup, that my lot was secure. I experienced that my boundary lines had fallen in pleasant places, and that I, too, had a delightful inheritance.

Do you believe the Father possesses all the resources of identity, love, pleasure, and place you need? Are you coming to him in faith, asking him to show you the full extent of your inheritance? As Frederick Buechner wrote, "If you have never known the power of God's love, then maybe it is because you have never asked to know it—I mean really asked, expecting an answer."[32]

By way of a quick recap, **identity** from the Father gives you *value*, **love** from the Father gives you *security*, **pleasure** from the Father gives you *motivation and energy*, and **place** from the Father gives you *honor*.

Think about how deeply your heart needs these four gifts. Remember how poorly these needs are filled by any substitute. And then, like my son Caleb did with me, run as fast as you can across the room toward your Father, holding nothing back and expecting only good in return. He longs to bless you beyond your highest expectations and fill you with his father's heart.

21

STREAMING THE HEART
OF GOD

Not long ago I was asked to speak at a seminar for leaders of family foundations on the impact father issues have on their lives. At the dinner that followed, a distinguished-looking, white-haired gentleman leaned across the table to introduce himself. It took only a few minutes of conversation to catch how bright and gifted this man was and sense the focused energy that had brought him such financial success.

But what he really wanted to talk to me about was his dad. "I'm seventy years old," he said, "and my dad is in his nineties. Yet whenever we are together it seems nothing has really changed. He still treats me like an incompetent boy." I nodded my head in understanding and began to ask how he typically responded. He brushed off my question and continued with even more intensity. "But what really bothers me is that my boys are in their mid-forties—and I treat them the same way. How can I break the chain?"

Most people immediately head in one of two directions when they begin to hear about a father's role in meeting their needs for identity, love, pleasure, and place. First they want to know how they can fix their dad, or at least repair their relationship with him. Second, they want to know how they can be the right kind of father to their children, or, in the case of wives, help their husband to be a good dad to their kids.

Many books have been written on the subject of repairing your relationship with your father, and many more have been written on how to be a good dad. Yet, if we start in either of those places, we run into the Law of Generations. This law is described and illustrated in a number of passages throughout the Bible (Exodus 20:5–6; 1 Kings 15:3; Romans 5:12). Basically we could summarize the Law of Generations by saying this: *Apart from the intervention of God, the sins of the father will be passed down to the next generation.*

Law of Generations

Sins of the Father   **2nd Generation**   **3rd Generation**

As you try to fix your dad or improve your relationship with him, you do so as one infected by the disease you are trying to cure. You will be distorted by your wounds, insulated by your self-protection, and skewed by your unmet needs. You will be impacted by the lies you have come to believe, be controlled by the idols you have come to worship, and feel self-justified by the unforgiveness you still harbor.

Your evaluation of the situation will not be accurate, since your senses will be amplified by pain or dulled by resignation. Perhaps most importantly, you will not see your dad through the eyes of *his* Father, who clearly sees the sin and is still moved with compassion. In fact, your attempts to help the situation might very well make it worse.

"Okay, I'll give up on Dad," you may conclude, "and concentrate on being a different kind of parent to my kids." Go for it.

I think you will find it more difficult than you realize. One boy described his dad's attempts to communicate love and pleasure as "a bad actor reading a script." He could feel that the lines were rehearsed and forced, and he sensed the true emotions of love and pleasure were not really there.

This is the problem with many how-to books on fathering. If your father issues are dealt with, their advice will be of great help. But if you skip your own healing, it will be like asking a paraplegic to practice the high jump. The capacity to perform will simply not be there. If you want a better relationship with your earthly father, begin by working through the process of healing that will properly connect you with your heavenly Father.

Then you can stream the resources of God back up the generational chain and be a blessing to your dad. The same is true in relationship to your children. The best way you can help them is to fill your heart up with the resources of the Father. Then, in a very natural way, you will be a channel of those resources to them.

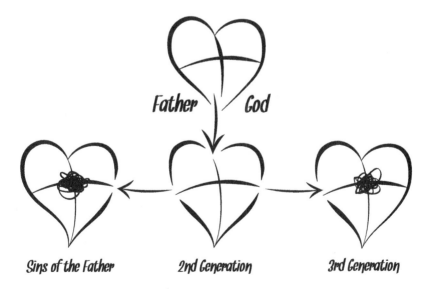

Father God

Sins of the Father   2nd Generation   3rd Generation

This is why we are addressing this subject now, at the end of the book, rather than at the beginning. Now that you have begun the work of awareness, cleansing, and restoration, you have the opportunity to stream the father heart of God to others. One of the first places it can go is back up the chain toward your earthly dad.

This does not mean you will father him. It does not mean you are responsible to fix him—remember, he has a Father who takes responsibility for that. It does mean you can fully step into your role as a son or daughter and stream identity, love, pleasure, and place back to him through that son or daughter "voice."

"Dad, I appreciate this about how God made you." "Dad, I love you." "Dad, I'm so proud of you, and I enjoy these things about you." "Dad, you are my earthly dad, and I honor you in that place." You have no idea how much a change in you can impact your relationship with him and flow back toward him with the redemptive power of Jesus.

Remember Julie's story in chapter 12? Her relationship with her dad was so broken that he would purposefully exclude her from family pictures and leave her out of reunion gatherings he initiated. Months and years would pass with no contact at all, and the few connections that did occur were forced and strained.

Not long after God led Julie through steps of healing to experience him as Father, her daughter became very ill. In a chain of events that could have only been orchestrated by God the Father, the doctor that could treat Julie's daughter was living in the same town as her dad. Needing a place to stay while she went through testing with her sick girl, Julie felt led to contact her dad—and his second wife—for help and a place to stay.

In the midst of this difficult trial, God surprised them all with his grace and love. The healing Julie had walked through made her heart open and compassionate toward her dad. The need to care for his daughter and her sick child opened up the father heart of Julie's dad. Sharing and asking questions they had never had the courage to voice, they sat around the dining room table talking till midnight for several nights in a row. Here is what happened next— in Julie's own words, written in a letter to a friend, which Julie graciously allowed me to reprint here:

> Then on Valentine's Day, when I opened my bedroom door that morning, I found a really sweet card signed by my dad. When roses were delivered to our house to me . . . from him . . . I stood in my room with tears running down my cheeks and realized . . . My Father has given me my father's heart. I know I am loved by him, thought about by him, and that he calls me his own. Oh my goodness, I can hardly even take it in now.
>
> But I have to write this so I don't ever forget. By making my heavenly Father's heart most important . . . looking to him and following him first . . . by making him my ultimate security . . . I won my father's heart. God's secret purpose framed from the beginning of this . . . to bring both my daughter and me . . . my whole family . . . to our full glory, is being fulfilled.

This is what is described in the very last verse of the Old Testament, Malachi 4:6: "He will turn the hearts of the parents to their children, and the hearts of the children to their parents." Did you catch the key phrase in Julie's letter? Her words jumped off the page when I first read them: *"By making my heavenly Father's heart most important . . . I won my father's heart."*

One of my joys has been to see this happen over and over again, in a myriad of supernatural ways. Remember Martina? I told you her story in chapter 11. You heard how she walked in the front door with a friend and suddenly learned her parents were getting a divorce and that she must choose between her mom and dad. You saw how the vow she made to not feel pain was blocking her from connecting with the love of God as an adult who had just put her trust in Jesus.

Several months after her breakthrough, I received this e-mail from her:

Dear friends,

Yesterday my dad told me he would come pick me up at the airport when I come home next month. We both don't really know how to communicate with each other . . . let alone express love. He didn't tell me: "I want to come pick you up." He was talking about my bag instead. "How big will your suitcase be? Will it be heavy?"

I told him it would be super-heavy, so . . . he is coming to get me! My dad who usually gives me a call on birthdays and Christmas and . . . that's it. And now he is going to drive so many miles to get me. He was the one to come up with this wonderful (!) idea. Wow!:) Yay!:) My dad is "crazy":) I don't think I can imagine that day, because it is such a wild dream . . . I can "only" live it. Aaaa!:) My relationship with dad has changed so much since we met for prayer. Thank you all again! God is miraculous!:) Martina

As soon as I read Martina's letter, I was moved to praise and worship. God is indeed miraculous!

You can stream the father heart of God up the chain toward your father, but you can also direct it down the chain toward your children. This begins an entirely new legacy, as the Law of Generations transmits a blessing instead of a curse.

Of all of the things I have learned about parenting, the most helpful has been the importance of receiving and channeling the heart of the heavenly Father toward my kids. This doesn't make me a perfect dad. On the contrary, failures are also an opportunity to model humility, ask for forgiveness, and redirect both of our eyes toward the source.

I have to remember that I am just a steward of my children—they really belong to God. In a very real way, I am parenting on behalf of the Father, and I need to be always asking what of his character, truth, and perspective I need to be passing on to them today. This all leads to a question some of you have already asked a number of times as you read these stories. "Hey, what about mothers? It sounds like you don't value them at all, since all you are talking about is the father! My mom had a huge influence in my life—and I want to influence my kids in the same way. Why don't you talk more about mothering?"

Good question. Mothers are hugely important and immensely valuable. They have a unique role of nurture and care in the life of a child that can't be replaced. I would never want to devalue that or downplay it—in fact, motherhood could easily be the topic of a similar book. I stand in awe at the amazing ways my wife, Connie, has been such a fabulous mother to our kids.

At the same time, there is an order to the universe. Within the Trinity, God reveals himself to us as Father and declares that all family is rooted in him (Ephesians 3:14–15). I believe the resources found in his father heart give context to all the other family roles: to those of mother, son, daughter, brother, sister, uncle, and aunt. A proper relationship with the Father provides the context and resources for all these other relationships to occur.

It is interesting to note that families with strong, loving fathers produce masculine boys *and* feminine girls. When the father presence is missing, both boys and girls tend to move toward neuter, losing the beauty and strength of their respective gender. In the same way, in the context of an engaged father, the mother is protected and released to fully function in her role of nurture and care. In the absence of this father presence, she naturally gravitates into his space to provide what is lacking, resulting in inadequate fathering and dysfunctional mothering. But what if the dad is not taking this role seriously or is missing altogether? What should the mom do in this case?

In a properly functioning chain of command, if someone does not fulfill his or her responsibilities, the burden of care moves up the chain rather than down. Because of this, the best thing a mother of fatherless children can do is place herself in proper relationship with her heavenly Father and ask him to fill the vacuum of fatherlessness that has been created. This is a responsibility God the Father takes very seriously. "A father to the fatherless, a defender of widows, is God in his holy dwelling. God sets the lonely in families, he leads out the prisoners with singing" (Psalm 68:5–6). Not only will God himself be a father to the fatherless, but he also will bring other resources to bear by setting "the lonely in families."

God will probably ask you to be one of these family members to someone else. Each of these family roles allows us to stream the father heart of God—his love, his pleasure, his identity, his place— to others in a different key. A melody that begins with the concert master can then be echoed by different instruments, in the key of brother or uncle or sister or daughter. Each of these family roles has a unique tone, but all of them can stream the father heart of God.

I can tell my brother how proud I am of him and reflect on how his Father must feel the same way. I can tell my daughter I love her and feel her heavenly Father's love for her as I say it. I can speak to a younger believer from the role of "uncle" as I remind him of the unique gifts and abilities God built into his life. At times I may be a surrogate father to one of God's adopted orphans, as I assure her she does, indeed, belong.

I've learned this melody needs to be playing in the background of every song; otherwise our attempts at music just produce dissonance. If I lead without tuning in to God's father heart, the oxygen goes out of the room and people are inevitably wounded by my attempts to shape and direct them.

If I serve without connecting with God's father heart, my actions come across as just dutiful and empty. If I preach without connecting with God's father heart, my words are missing both his power and his presence. And if I try to help others without leading them to the Father, I have very little to offer.

Maintaining your connection with God's father heart and continuing to deepen your understanding of his father care will affect every area of your life. That is why Jesus talked so much about the Father in his last conversation with his disciples before he was crucified, when they were together in the upper room. He was about to leave them, but first he promised, "I will not leave you as orphans" (John 14:18). He assured them, "I am in my Father, and you are in me, and I am in you" (John 14:20). Then he made this promise: "Anyone who loves me will obey my teaching. My Father will love them, and we will come to them and make our home with them" (John 14:23).

If the disciples needed those words to be ready for the challenges ahead of them, we certainly still need them today. When you know the Father's love, you have protection and safety that cannot be shaken by the worst life can throw at you. And when the Father and the Son make their home with you, their presence will spread life and blessing to everyone around you.

22

BETTER THAN YOU KNOW

On July 5, 1687, Sir Isaac Newton upended the scientific world with the publication of his *Mathematical Principles of Natural Philosophy*, or *Principia*, as it came to be known. With brilliant insight, Newton pulled back the curtain on a wide range of phenomena we observe in the world around us, giving us the theory of gravitation, the mathematics behind the movement of planets, and a powerful explanation of moving objects, known today as Newton's laws of motion.

You may remember his three laws of motion from your high school physics class, because they form the basis for any study of objects that move. The first law defines a force Newton calls *inertia*, which is defined as "a power of resisting, by which every body, as much as in it lies, endeavors to preserve its present state, whether it be of rest, or of moving uniformly forward in a right line."[33] In layman's terms, inertia is a natural resistance to change built into everything that has mass. In order to overcome it, external force must be applied.

What does this have to do with the fatherhood of God?

Actually, a great deal.

The fact that you have read this far says a lot. Either you are one of those people who must, by principle, finish every book you start, or you have a genuine interest in a deeper connection with God. In either case, I commend you! In spite of this, I know the law of inertia is working against you. Your natural tendency will be to read these final pages, close the back cover, and continue in the same direction as you were headed before, at the same speed as you were going before, with the same results as you had before. You, like me, naturally resist change.

I know from experience if you do the hard work of awareness, cleansing, and restoration in relationship to God as Father, the results will be profoundly life changing. I also know how easy it is to nod and do nothing, agree and put it off, or come up with some good excuse—"not me," "later," or "someday." You need an external force to jar you out of inertia and change your trajectory. I'm hoping to prod you with my words, but I have much more hope in two forces that are being brought to bear right now, whether you are aware of them or not.

One is a "push"; the other is a "pull."

Let your mind run quickly through the events of the last two weeks. Is there anything poking you right now, causing discomfort and leaving you unsettled? Are you facing some problems that won't go away, health challenges that you can't resolve, or conflicts that are weighing you down? Are there issues burning loops in your mind, circling over and over again because you can't seem to find the answer?

The Bible clearly teaches that trials and difficulties form powerful tools God uses to accomplish our sanctification. They press on us, jar us, disturb our natural state of stagnation. They poke and prod. We poke back, trying to push them off, force them away, and return to our state of rest. We view them as intruders, as enemies. Could trials and difficulties actually be your allies and friends, sent by God as an external force to help you overcome your built-in resistance to change?

Think back to what is poking or prodding you right now. Instead of just pushing back, can you ask the question, "What is

God pushing on?" If a recent event has you locked down in fear, you know now the Father's love will provide safety. If you are unable to enter that safe place, you can ask the Counselor to show you why (awareness), and he may take you back to the origins of your mistrust in defining moments from the past. Then you can ask the Holy Spirit to reveal any things that need to be cleansed (US LIV—unforgiveness, sin, lies, idolatry, vows), and you can respond with prayers of repentance and faith.

Praying the prayers of Ephesians for yourself, you can ask for "the Spirit of wisdom and revelation" so you would know the Father better (restoration) and then wait on him to reveal himself into that place. The result could be a supernatural encounter with the love of your Father, one that gives you safety in spite of your circumstances. Your trial could actually be a gift, the key to a door that unlocks more of your inheritance.

If a conversation from this week has you feeling insecure about who you are, you can remember that your identity and place are defined by your Father in a perfect and wholly adequate way. You can seek this truth in his Word and ask for confirmation from his Spirit, who testifies with your spirit that you are his son or daughter. If you can't hear or receive this message, ask the Counselor why (awareness). Then let him search your heart to see if anything needs to be cleansed. He may show you something in the present (unforgiveness, sin, lies, idolatry, vows) or take you back to a defining moment from the past.

Once you have responded to his illumination with repentance and faith, you can pray the father prayers of Ephesians and wait on him in faith for an answer. That threatening conversation may have shown that your identity and place were not anchored in the solid rock of your Father's heart. Your response to this trial could lead you to an even deeper encounter with his power and grace.

I spent much of today at the hospital, meeting with an orthopedic specialist and helping my wife through an extensive MRI. During both the appointment and the testing, she was debilitated by nausea and blinding pain from a migraine that started in the middle of the night. This has been her third migraine in four weeks, on top of chronic pain in her shoulder and numbness in her arm. The tests today came back inconclusive. The doctors have no idea what is wrong.

I hate watching my wife suffer—especially when there is no clear solution in sight. I want to rescue her, to make it right, and I don't know how. She is worn out from discomfort and pain. I am weary of not knowing what to do. I had planned to write all day, but the Father had a different plan. This trial has been poking me every minute of today and during much of the last two weeks as I've labored on the last chapters you read. It seems to me like a painful interruption, a diversion from God's good plan.

However, I know that my Father is in control and that he is working in all things for my good. That good is conformity to the image of his Son (Romans 8:28–29). My Father knows I am deeply impacted by the law of inertia—the tendency to stay where I am. Today I feel the "power of resisting" that Newton described in his law. But this trial provides an external force, a "push" that can, if I allow, lead me to new encounters with his father heart.

That is what I am praying for today.

Thankfully, there is also a second force, a "pull" that works to change my trajectory and increase my velocity. It is energized by the Spirit, who is always testifying to my spirit, and by Jesus, who is always opening the way, and by the Father, who is always drawing me to himself. In their "pull" is a constant call to something more, to something I was made for but have only partially tasted. As they pull, a voice of false comfort resists, telling me I have reached my goal and have already arrived at my destination. "You already know the Father," the voice whispers soothingly, "and have already received what he wants to give you. You are in a good spot now. Remember, you have already experienced sanctification and healing."

When challenged, this voice of false comfort responds belligerently: "Are you telling me that you haven't received anything from the Father, that you haven't grown, that you don't know him at all?" When I pay attention to this voice, I am tempted to conclude, "I can stop now. No need to move forward; no need to continue to grow."

Every gift that you have received is yours, every battle won is a true victory, and every step of growth becomes a part of who you are. But do you really want to stop? That would be like saying at the end of a meal, "That was so amazing, I think I will never eat again," or concluding at the end of a great date with your spouse, "Now we know everything about each other. I guess we don't need to talk anymore." While darkness can be absolute, light can always get brighter. Goodness can always increase. Joy can always be richer. You can never plumb the depths of the wealth of almighty God.

Do you really want to stop?

That is why Paul wrote, "Not that I have already obtained all this, or have already arrived at my goal, but *I press on* to take hold of that for which Christ Jesus took hold of me" (Philippians 3:12, emphasis added). I'm not there yet—what a glorious thought! This means it can keep getting better! "And we all, who with unveiled faces contemplate the Lord's glory, are being transformed into his image with *ever-increasing glory*, which comes from the Lord, who is the Spirit" (2 Corinthians 3:18, emphasis added).

Do you feel a bit restless or unsatisfied? Do you want more? This is the pull of the Spirit, telling you about your inheritance, the pull of Jesus, leading you to the Father, the pull of the Father himself, drawing you into more of the fullness of what he has to offer.

Become more aware of these longings and desires—and let them pull you out of inertia into a closer encounter with God.

"Indeed, if we consider the unblushing promises of reward and the staggering nature of the rewards promised in the Gospels," wrote C. S. Lewis, "it would seem that Our Lord finds our desires, not too strong, but too weak. We are half-hearted creatures, fooling about with drink and sex and ambition when infinite joy is offered us, like an ignorant child who wants to go on making mud pies in a slum because he cannot imagine what is meant by the offer of a holiday at the sea. We are far too easily pleased."[34]

I'm prodding you with my words. Take the truths you have learned about the father heart of God and start doing the hard personal work that will bring lasting transformation. Don't turn this last page and walk away. The trials and difficulties you experienced this week are pushing you. Take note of where the pressures are. Welcome them from your loving Father, and let them drive you to him. Your longings and desires are pulling you—because you were made for so much more. Listen through them to hear God's voice, and don't be satisfied with mud pies in a slum. The Father is waiting.

He is better than you know.

SUMMARY

The process of father redemption involves three steps — *Awareness, Cleansing* and *Restoration*

Awareness

The four gifts of the Father represent core needs that cry out from every human heart:

1. Identity
2. Love
3. Pleasure
4. Place

The Father's Heart

We hear God the Father give these gifts to his Son at Jesus' baptism (Matthew 3:17) and transfiguration (Matthew 17:5). Jesus used the four gifts as his defense when attacked by the Jewish leaders, giving us great insight into his experience of God's father heart (John 5:16–44).

"This is my Son, whom I love; with him I am well pleased. Listen to him!"
(Matthew 17:5)

Identity from the Father gives you **value**.
Love from the Father gives you **security**.
Pleasure from the Father gives you **motivation and energy**.
Place from the Father gives you **honor**.

Our earthly fathers were meant to imprint us with these four gifts. They are to be filled up in relationship with our heavenly Father. Because of sin, our father's imprint is never clean. If your dad is your hero, you may subconsciously conclude you don't need another dad or make God "dad-sized," which is a box way too small for him. If your dad is your heartache, he can fill your heart with disappointment and debris, leaving no space for a Dad of a different kind.

Each of us receives a combination of three things from our earthly fathers:

1. Father gifts
2. Father wounds
3. Father vacuums

If we observe our behavior, we can spot these three by their corresponding symptoms:

1. Father gifts produce **giving** and **receiving**.
2. Father vacuums produce **deadness** (the corpse) and **pulls** (the vacuum cleaner).
3. Father wounds produce **self-protection** (armor) and **distortion** (the amplifier).

Any or all of these symptoms can be present in each of the four chambers of our hearts.

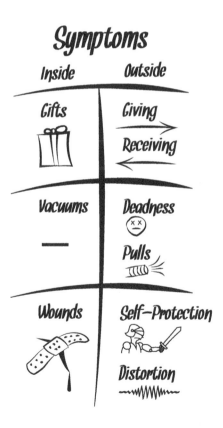

Father mapping can help you do a quick diagnostic of the four areas of your heart, showing the extent of father gifts, father wounds, and father vacuums in each area.

Cleansing

Once we know where we have deficiencies, it would seem logical just to go to our heavenly Father and have these needs met. Our experience, however, tells us his gifts will often bounce off and not penetrate. Why is that? Because what looks to be empty is actually full. In absence of the Father's resources, five common heart diseases have taken root. You will need the help of the Counselor, the Holy Spirit, to reveal these to you.

Since these diseases are often rooted in **defining moments** from the past, it is very helpful to ask the Counselor to reveal these memories to you. Often these defining moments provide the key to diagnosing and cleansing the disease that is preventing your heart from being healed. These five common diseases of the heart can be remembered by US LIV—he wants "us" to "liv."

1. **Unforgiveness** – Matthew 18:21–35
2. **Sin** – Isaiah 53:1–6; 1 John 1:5—2:1
3. **Lies** – John 8:44
4. **Idolatry** – Jeremiah 17:1–8
5. **Vows** – Isaiah 30:1–18

Each of these diseases is cleansed through **repentance** and **faith** (Mark 1:15).

Restoration

You must first understand the key roles of Jesus and the Holy Spirit. Jesus reveals the Father in flesh and is the only way to him

(John 14:6). When you put your trust in him, he invites you to join his relationship with the Father (John 14:9–20). The Spirit testifies with your spirit that you belong to God, leads you to call out, "*Abba*, Father," and helps you receive your inheritance (Romans 8:14–17). There are two father prayers in Ephesians that are key to restoration:

1. The prayer for "the Spirit of wisdom and revelation" (Ephesians 1:15–22)
2. The prayer for the power to know a "love that surpasses knowledge" (Ephesians 3:14–19)

As we seek the Father, he can fill each of these key areas of our heart, revealing himself to us in a real and personal way.

1. **Identity**
   Psalm 139:13–15
   Ephesians 1:1–14

2. **Love**
   Romans 5:8
   Romans 8:31–32
   Romans 8:37
   Ephesians 3:17–19
   1 John 3:1

3. **Pleasure**
   1 Samuel 15:22
   Psalm 51:16–17
   Zephaniah 3:17
   John 8:28–29

2 Corinthians 5:9–10
Ephesians 1:4–5
Ephesians 1:8–9
2 Timothy 2:3–4
Hebrews 11:6

4. **Place**
Genesis 1:28–29
Psalm 16:5–6
Psalm 139:16
John 14:2
Ephesians 2:10

Because of this restoration, we can stream the father heart of God up the generational chain to our fathers and down the chain to our children. We can also play the melody of his heart in the key of sister, brother, uncle, or aunt. We should never stop growing in our knowledge of him—light can always get brighter.

The Father Diagnostic

1. **Identity** – John 5:16–19
Who am I? Am I valuable? Do I have to be just like you to be significant? Am I competent? Capable?

Without identity from the Father, you will be defined by the people and circumstances around you. This will be constantly changing and unstable. You will be very vulnerable to your environment and not have a clear sense of self. You will constantly need to either prove yourself or defend yourself. In fact, here's how your thinking will be warped:

- Instead of "I failed," you think, "I am a failure."
- Instead of "They are disappointed," you think, "I am disappointing."
- Instead of "It didn't work; I have to try again," you think, "I am incapable."
- Instead of "That wasn't worthwhile," you think, "I am worthless."
- Instead of "Your opinion is important," you think, "I am what you think of me."

2. **Love** — John 5:20

Am I loved unconditionally? Am I precious and treasured to someone? Do I matter to anyone? Does someone care deeply about me? Do I feel and hear your love and affection?

Without receiving the Father's love, you will be constantly trying to gain love from those near you. Their love will never be enough, and you will be chronically disappointed. You may cope by turning off your emotions and becoming distant and cold. Without the knowledge that you are well loved by God, here's what happens:

- You will have a hard time trusting love.
- Love may not penetrate your heart.
- Your relationships will become consumed with getting rather than giving.
- You will have a hard time giving love to others.

3. **Pleasure** — John 5:30, 41–44

Are you proud of me? Do you delight in me? Are you pleased with who I am? Do you enjoy my presence? Do you like being with me? Do I bring you joy?

Without pleasure from the Father, you will become addicted to pleasing people and vulnerable to hedonism. You may cope by avoiding all possibility of failure or rejection.

- You could be easily addicted to almost anything—food, alcohol, money, clothes, sex, adrenaline, unhealthy relationships.
- On the other hand, you may be passionless, without excitement, dead to joy and healthy pleasure.
- You may exhibit a great deal of avoidance behavior—not to maximize gain, but minimize loss. It is easier not to try than to try and fail.
- Disappointment from others will be toxic for you.

4. **Place** – John 5:21–27

Do I have purpose? Does my life matter? Is there some place that is uniquely mine? Do I fit? Do I belong? Am I a part of something bigger than myself? Do I have something to give? Would you notice if I were gone?

Without a place from your Father, you will be constantly fighting to make a place for yourself. You will fear your life has no significance and be easily threatened by others. You may cope by scaling back your expectations and making a place that is small but defensible—like when people curl up in a ball, hide behind something, or retreat to a corner. Here's what you'll experience without a sense of place:

- You will be restless and easily distracted by "greener grass."
- You will not be confident in your role.
- You may feel threatened by others who are secure.
- You will shrink back from your God-given responsibilities.
- You will overreact to criticism.

- You may use power plays to defend your space.
- You will feel a constant need to prove yourself.

How to walk through the steps of awareness, cleansing and restoration

1. Ask a friend or your spouse to set aside time to think and pray with you about a deeper connection with God's father heart. If that is not possible, reserve a time and place to be alone and journal your thoughts. Make that journal your dialogue partner.

2. Tell them (or your journal) which of the four areas (identity, love, pleasure and place) you want to make progress in, and share the symptoms you are seeing. Ask for their feedback and observations, or record your own.

3. Then share with them (or your journal friend) the defining moments God has brought to mind as you have thought and prayed about this. Stop, pray, and ask the Spirit if there are any others that are important to add.

4. Pray that God the Father will transform these areas so you will be able to connect with all the resources he has for you.

5. Ask the Father to show you through his Spirit which of the defining moments he wants you to start with. If you don't have a clear sense, start with the one that occurred first in your life.

6. Pray that the Holy Spirit would take you back to this moment in your mind and show you what needs to be cleansed so the Father's gifts can fill this place. Ask Jesus to bring his light to this experience and to reveal his person and work into this memory. Make sure you take the time to listen after you pray.

7. Go through the list of the five common heart diseases—US LIV. Ask the Spirit to show you if any of these were formed in this defining moment or in the pattern of experiences that it represents. As he reveals these to you, cleanse them with repentance and faith.

8. Here is how repentance and faith are expressed with each of these diseases:

- **Unforgiveness** – Repent of unforgiveness, calling it sin; and, in faith, forgive as Christ forgave you.
- **Sin** – If it is your sin, name it just as Jesus names it (don't deceive yourself), and ask him to forgive and cleanse you. If it is someone else's sin against you, turn from trying to bear that yourself, and in faith place it on the cross. Ask Jesus to take that burden and poison from you.
- **Lies** – Name the lie and declare in prayer that it is not true. Reject it as false and something you will not continue to believe. In faith, accept the truth. Declare in prayer that you believe the truth to be true and that you desire to live out of that truth.
- **Idolatry** – Name the idol and renounce it by calling it a false god that has no power to save you. In prayer, destroy the idol by defiling it and symbolically grinding it to dust. In faith, place the true God in its place, committing your alliance to him and pledging to turn to him instead of to the idol.
- **Vows** – Renounce the vow and break it in the name of Jesus. Declare that it was a godless vow because it did not include God but represented your own effort to secure protection. In faith, make a new vow, asking

the Holy Spirit for the words that he wants you to use. This vow will be a vow to trust God and turn to him, relying on him for protection and salvation.

9. Generally, each defining moment will have several of the heart diseases, so continue to ask the Holy Spirit to reveal them until he assures you that your work there is finished. Then pray again for God's father presence to fill this place with his gifts to you. Make sure you stop and receive them, taking special note of what he is saying to you through his Spirit, through his Son, and through his Scriptures.

10. When that memory is finished, ask the Spirit which is the next one he wants you to deal with. Move on to that defining moment, and go back through steps 6–10.

11. When you are finished with what the Lord wants you to deal with in this time of prayer, make sure you thank him for what he has done. Seal it by affirming again that you believe and receive what he has given to you.

12. Write down what the Lord showed you and the decisions you made. It will further solidify his work and help you recall the details in the future. This is important, because sometimes the change is so radical and complete that it is even hard to remember how you felt before the Father cleansed that area of your heart!

ACKNOWLEDGMENTS

No journey of any magnitude should be attempted alone, and I would have never finished this project without the gracious and willing help of others. My first of word of thanks goes to the Josiah Venture team who allowed me to teach the initial draft of this material to them at a spring staff conference, and then gave me several years of feedback and stories once the event was finished. Thanks for being such an amazingly gifted team, and always ready to reach for more in your personal relationships with God. You are the greatest!

I'm so grateful to the Josiah Venture board who allowed me to take an extended sabbatical to focus on research and writing, and didn't give away my job while I was gone. You are a constant source of wisdom and feedback to me, and always thinking about how to further God's kingdom. I can't believe I get to serve under your leadership.

Mel Ellenwood and Brian Stephens, you are amazing ministry partners and so gracious to carry the full load of leadership responsibilities for JV while I was diving deep into the complexities of God's father heart. I love serving Jesus with the two of you!

Bob and Sherry, Steve and Polly, you both offered your homes to Connie and I at key times for extended periods of study and writing. I'm praying that your generosity will ripple out to bless many. Thanks for believing in both of us and loving us in such practical ways.

To Daryle Doden and the team at Ambassador, you both took a real risk in beta testing this material with a number of your key friends, and then were courageously direct in your feedback, both positive and critical. Your initiative and foresight were used by God to open the way. Thank you.

Chris Hudson of Hudson Bible, thank you for your tireless and wise management of the entire project, and Bob DeMoss for your careful and insightful editorial work. Your tremendous depth of experience and skill were invaluable to a rookie like me. I am deeply grateful.

I am so thankful to the many who allowed me to tell their stories. You were courageous and vulnerable. I pray many will be blessed because of your willingness to share your journeys with the Father.

Then there are those who have faithfully modeled God's father heart to me through their investment into my life. Dann Spader, Charlie Bradshaw, Rich Kerns (who got to the Father's house ahead of the rest of us) and Philip Vierling. Each of you has shaped my understanding of the Father in so many practical and transformational ways.

More than from any other man, I've learned about God's Father heart from my earthly dad, Dick Patty. Thanks for being such a man of the Word, for being transparently imperfect, and yet still such a powerful channel of God's Father heart to me. I'm so glad you are still here to read this!

Tyler, Caleb and Claire Patty, all three of you bring me such joy! Thanks for putting up with an imperfect dad, for making fathering such a fun and rich adventure, and for teaching me so much of God's Father heart just by letting me be your father. I love who each of you have become, and look forward to many more years of being family together!

Connie, you are the love of my life and my favorite friend. Thanks for walking this long journey together, letting me pound on my keyboard for hours on end, and always being willing to read and respond, encourage and redirect. Your faith and sacrifice got me through!

Finally, and most importantly, to Jesus Christ, who gave his life so he could make a way for me to enter into a relationship with his Father, and now mine. Eternity will not be enough to express the gratitude and praise that He deserves.

NOTES

1   Sarah Allen, PhD, and Kerry Daly, PhD, "The Effects of Father Involvement: An Updated Research Summary of the Evidence," Father Involvement Research Alliance, University of Guelph, May 2007, http://www.fira.ca/cms/documents/29/Effects_of_Father_Involvement.pdf.

2   Margo Maine, PhD (2010-02-01). *Father Hunger: Fathers, Daughters, and the Pursuit of Thinness* (Kindle Locations 262–263). Gürze Books. Kindle Edition.

3   Ibid.

4   Jonathan Van Meter, "Adele: One and Only," *Vogue*, February 13, 2012, http://www.vogue.com/magazine/article/adele-one-and-only/#1.

5   Caroline Goddard, "Adele's Father Proves Her Point," SheKnows.com, February 20, 2012, http://www.sheknows.com/entertainment/articles/950489/adeles-father-proves-her-point.

6   Claire Hoffman, "On the Cover: Drake," *GQ*, April 13, 2012, http://www.gq.com/story/drake-interview-gq-april-2012.

7   James L. Schaller, *The Search for Lost Fathering: Rebuilding Your Father Relationship* (Fleming H Revell Co,1995).

8   Ibid.

9   J. Randy Taraborrelli, *Michael Jackson: The Magic, the Madness, the Whole Story, 1958–2009* (New York: Grand Central Publishing, 2009), 612.

10   Campbell Brown interview with Rabbi Shmuley Boteach, CNN, June 30, 2009, http://www.cnn.com/2009/SHOWBIZ/Music/06/30/jackson.rabbi/index.html?iref=24hours.

11   John Calvin, *Institutes of Christian Religion*, I.XI.8.

12   Fred Craddock, *Craddock Stories* (St. Louis: Chalice Press, 2001), 156–157.

13   Quoted from the "About Us" page at Lifewithoutlimbs.org, http://www.lifewithoutlimbs.org/about-life-without-limbs/.

14   Ann Tatlock, *The Returning* (Bloomington, MN: Bethany House Publishers, 2009), 268.

15   Frederick Buechner, *The Magnificent Defeat*, reprint ed. (New York: HarperCollins, 1985), 135.

16   C. S. Lewis, *The Problem of Pain* (MacMillan,1976), 46–47.

17   Brennan Manning, *The Ragamuffin Gospel: Good News for the Bedraggled, Beat-Up, and Burnt Out* (Colorado Springs: Multnomah Books, 2008).

18   Martin Luther, *On Christian Liberty*, 1520.

19   William R. Moody, *The Life of Dwight L. Moody* (Albany, OR: Books for the Ages/Ages Software, 1997), 127.

20   "Desmond Tutu, Insisting We Are 'Made for Goodness,' "
NPR.org, March 11, 2010, http://www.npr.org/templates/story/story.
php?storyId=124539592.

21   Linda Anderson, "An Open Letter to Family Men," *Our Daily Bread*,
1989.

22   Aria Shahrokhshahi, "The Day I Passed Maths," original YouTube
video, October 21, 2013, https://www.youtube.com/watch?v=Ls9Cg8iaq1s.

23   Scott Stump, "Father from Viral Math Video: 'I Was
Overwhelmed,' " *TODAY*, October 23, 2013, http://www.today.com/news/
father-viral-math-video-i-was-overwhelmed-8C11447428.

24   Aria Shahrokhshahi, "The Day I Passed Maths," original
YouTube video, October 21, 2013, http://www.youtube.com/
watch?feature=player_embedded&v=Ls9Cg8iaq1s.

25   Charles Sell, *Unfinished Business: Helping Adult Children Resolve Their Past*
(Colorado Springs: Multnomah, 1989), 171ff.

26   D. P. Thomson, *Scotland's Greatest Athlete: The Eric Liddell Story* (Crieff,
Perthshire: The Research Unit, 1970), accessed from "Quotes by and about Eric
Liddell from D P Thomson's 'Scotland's Greatest Athlete,' " The Eric Liddell
Centre, http://www.ericliddell.org/ericliddell/quotations.

27   Ibid.

28   Dr. Norman Maclean, *The Scotsman*, July 19, 1924, in D. P. Thomson,
Scotland's Greatest Athlete: The Eric Liddell Story (Crieff, Perthshire: The Research
Unit, 1970), accessed from "Quotes by and about Eric Liddell from D P
Thomson's 'Scotland's Greatest Athlete,' " The Eric Liddell Centre, http://
www.ericliddell.org/ericliddell/quotations.

29   Bob Smietana, "Running Out of Miracles," *Christianity Today*, May 1,
2004, http://www.christianitytoday.com/ct/2004/may/4.44.html?start=1.

30   Diane Wakoski, "The Father of My Country" from *Emerald Ice: Selected
Poems 1962-1987*. Copyright © 1988 by Diane Wakoski. Reprinted with the
permission of Black Sparrow Books, an imprint of David R. Godine, Publisher,
Inc.

31   Bob Smietana, "Running Out of Miracles," *Christianity Today*, May 1,
2004, http://www.christianitytoday.com/ct/2004/may/4.44.html?start=3.

32   Frederick Buechner, *The Magnificent Defeat*, reprint ed. (New York:
HarperCollins, 1985).

33   Isaac Newton, *Principia: The Mathematical Principles of Natural Philosophy*,
translated by Andrew Motte (New York: Daniel Adee, 1848), 73.

34   C. S. Lewis, *The Weight of Glory* (New York: HarperOne, 2001), 26.

Made in the USA
Monee, IL
28 July 2022

10463148R00144